Moll Flanders

A musical

Book by Claire Luckham

Lyrics by Paul Leigh
(Original lyrics by Claire Luckham and Chris Bond)

Music by George Stiles
(Based on tunes of the period)

Based on the novel by Daniel Defoe

Samuel French — London
New York - Toronto - Hollywood

MOLL FLANDERS

Presented at the Lyric Theatre, Hammersmith, on 28th
April 1993 with the following cast:

Moll Flanders	Josie Lawrence
Nurse, Corrinder, Daisy,	
Angel, Publican's Wife, Whore	Issy Van Randwyck
Lady Constable, Barmaid,	
Bank Clerk, Mother Midnight	Angela Richards
Elizabeth, Lucie, Bank Clerk,	
Angel, Child, Whore	Clare Burt
Luke, Gambler, Abe,	
Bank Clerk, Jemmy, Boy	Vincent Leigh
Man in Gaol, Cyril, Publican,	
Sycophant, Bank Clerk, Priest	Darryl Knock
Mayor of Colchester, Ralph,	
Drunkard, Biggins, Bank Clerk,	
Angel, Scotsman	Martyn Ellis
Jailer, Artist, Henry, Lord,	
Mr Honest, Tradesman	David Tysall
Robert, Fornicator, Jerry, Landlord,	
Bank Clerk, Angel, Judge	Peter Woodward

Directed by Peter James
Designed by Sally Crabb
Lighting by Hugh Vanstone
Musical Direction by Tony Castro
Musical Staging by Gillian Gregory
Sound by John Del'Nero
Musical Arrangements by Mark Warman

SYNOPSIS OF SCENES AND MUSICAL NUMBERS

ACT I

SCENE 1	Opening	
Song 1	**Let Us Tell a Tale**	Company
SCENE 2	Newgate Gaol	
Song 2	**Lullaby**	Elizabeth
SCENE 3	Chorus Scene	
Song 3	**A Baby**	Chorus
SCENE 4	Colchester	
Song 4	**Moll's Prayer**	Moll
SCENE 5	Lady Constable's Home	
Song 5	**Portrait Song**	Artist, Lady Constable, Cyril, Robert, Corrinder, Moll
SCENE 6	The Same	
Song 6	**The Seduction**	Moll, Lady Constable, Cyril, Corrinder, Robert
SCENE 7	The Same	
Song 7	**Her Love Made Her Rich**	Chorus, Moll
SCENE 8	London	
Song 8	**The Masque**	Luke, Moll, Ralph, Henry
SCENE 9	The Mint	
Song 9	**The Mint**	Gambler, Drunkard, Fornicator
SCENE 10	A quayside public house and its environs	
Song 10	**A Sailor's Life**	Abe, Jerry, Barmaid
Song 11	**Lap-dogs**	Moll, Lucie, Abe, Jerry

Music

The music for *Moll Flanders* is available from Samuel French Ltd.

CHARACTERS

Elizabeth, Moll's mother
Woman
Man
Mayor of Colchester
Nurse
Moll Flanders
Lady Constable
Corrinder
Robert
Cyril
Artist
Luke
Ralph
Henry
Gambler
Drunkard
Fornicator
Lucie
Abe
Jerry
Barmaid
Publican
Sycophant
Lord
Biggins
Wife
Priest
Daisy
Landlord
Clerk
Honest
Jemmy
Mother Midnight
Publican's Wife
Child
Tradesman
Fop
Judge
Boy
Girl
Chorus, Londoners, Ladies and **Gentlemen,** etc.

Moll Flanders can be performed effectively by a cast of nine (four women and five men). The doubling suggested below (covering the principal roles) was used in the Lyric Theatre, Hammersmith production in 1993.

Female 1 Moll Flanders

Female 2 Corrinder, Nurse, Daisy, Publican's Wife, Ensemble

Female 3 Lady Constable, Mother Midnight, Mad Wife, Ensemble

Female 4 Elizabeth, Moll's Mother, Lucie, Child, Ensemble

Male 1 Luke, Abe, Jemmy, Boy, Ensemble

Male 2 Man in Gaol, Cyril, Publican, Priest, Ensemble

Male 3 Mayor of Colchester, Ralph, Biggins, Clerk, Fop, Ensemble

Male 4 Artist, Henry, Honest, Tradesman, Ensemble

Male 5 Robert, Jerry, Landlord, Judge, Ensemble

ACT I

Scene 1

Song 1: Let Us Tell a Tale

Company   Let us tell a tale
Of adventure and ambition
Of an island and its mission
As an empire comes to pass
And the tall ships sail
To barter, trade and tender
And all for the great splendour
Of the English merchant class

But turn your face
From this glory that is risen
Our story starts in prison
Where the stoutest heart must fail
For there's a place
Of shame and degradation
At the hub of this mighty nation
And its name is Newgate Gaol

For what can be the cure
For the armies of the poor
But the judges and the Bridewell
And the shadow of the noose?
For what the law prohibits
There is wood enough for gibbets
And for every one that's tried, well
It's a good enough excuse
That the dead don't reproduce
No, the dead don't reproduce

So lend an ear
To a tale of market forces
Of dowries and divorces

In a land where all's for sale
Where bread is dear
But life is sold more cheaply
And no road descends as steeply
As the road to Newgate Gaol

Let us lift the veil
On a woman's desperate measures
In a world of carnal pleasures
Where the bold alone prevail
Let us tell a tale
Of money, sex and slanders
The history of Moll Flanders
It begins in Newgate Gaol

Let us tell a tale
Of death's head grins
And mortal sins
It begins in Newgate Gaol

There is a crossfade to:

SCENE 2

Newgate Gaol

Elizabeth Wright is on her knees. Woman and Man are in semi-darkness

Elizabeth I, Elizabeth Wright, a woman without a future, have been condemned to death by hanging by the neck. My crime? The theft of a roll of cloth from a draper's shop. Dear God, I'm hardly twenty, don't let me die!

Woman Shut up, will you. It's the same for all of us. We don't need it rammed down our throats.

Elizabeth Sir! Help me!

Man Don't talk stupid. I'd help meself if I could, but this hole's lousy with iron bars and locks; even the windows are in the bleedin' ceiling. And suppose we did get out — how are we going to get past the soddin' jailers, eh?

Elizabeth Take me.

Man Where to, for God's sake? I've just explained ...

Elizabeth No. *Take* me. Get me pregnant as fast as you can. They can't hang me if I'm pregnant. It's the law.

Man Well, anything to do with the law's expensive ...
Elizabeth How much?
Man What have you got?
Elizabeth This.

She produces a gold coin. Man takes it and bites it

Man Right.
Elizabeth (*aside*) Ladies and gentlemen, sex as a dire necessity. A necessity
  my daughter will come to know all about.
Man Excuse us, ladies and gentlemen. Talk amongst yourselves.

*Elizabeth bends over. Man lifts her skirt and stands behind her. Neither of
them move. Man looks about him, bored, and whistles a verse of the march
from Handel's* Rinaldo

Elizabeth (*standing up*) Thank you.
Man Happy to oblige. Over and above the money involved, I enjoyed that.
  If it doesn't take, I'd even consider giving you a discount next time.

He exits

The introduction to Song 2 begins

Elizabeth I am saved! And not just for nine months, for while I am pleading
  my belly my sentence is commuted to transportation. They need labour in
  the colonies. Praise be to God!

Man enters and hands Elizabeth a baby

Man And man.

He exits

Elizabeth She is a beautiful baby. All there, every bit of her; each little finger,
  each little toe, all complete.

Song 2: Lullaby

(*Singing*) Sleep, my pretty, but, oh, for pity
Never ask who it was gave you birth

> The moon shines pale and the cold winds wail
> And I must sail to the ends of the earth
>
> So guard your virtue from those who'd hurt you
> Keep your foot from the slippery slope
> That leads to sadness, grief and madness
> And the end of the hangman's rope

(*Speaking*) The only pity is I can't take you with me, not to the penal colony in Virginia where I'm bound. Poor baby, I've got to leave you to fend for yourself.

> To go may grieve me, but please believe me
> Few can show better reasons than I
> Who will guide you, stand beside you
> Watch you grow as the seasons go by?
>
> God above me, if you love me
> Fill this child with the light of your hope
> Keep her close and keep her always
> Keep her from the hangman's rope

(*Speaking*) Here's a note to pin on you. (*She extracts the note and reads*) "Look after my baby. Elizabeth Wright."

> The drums are beating
> Life is fleeting
> Take care
> Beware
> The hangman's rope

There is a crossfade and the scene dissolves to:

Scene 3

The company are on stage, passing Elizabeth's baby around

Song 3: A Baby

Company   A baby's a curse
                     That'll lighten your purse
                     The one thing it'll bring you is sorrow

For all that she may look so sweet for today
She'll be meat for the gallows tomorrow
If you want to raise something that's useful
Try raising some money instead
Why bother to breed when it's bread that you need
And you can't even feed what you've bred

A baby, a baby, another guttersnipe
A baby, a baby, another snotty nose to wipe

Though passion and vice
May be all very nice
There's a price if the oven's a hot one
And charity's said to begin in the home
So forget it if you haven't got one
An orphan's a bundle of trouble
An orphan is better off drowned
For each seed that you sow, there's a weed that may grow
And there's only so much to go round

A baby, a baby, a bag of wind and sick
A baby, a baby, another bloody arse to kick

A baby's a curse
And a female is worse
All her life all she'll know of is sorrow
She'll be there on her back in the poorhouse today
On her back in the whore-house tomorrow
When you think what's in store for a baby
It's pointless to preach or pretend
When they die premature you may cry, to be sure
But we've all got to go in the end

A baby, a baby, a recipe for strife
A baby, a baby, another bleeding wasted life

Well, babies may grow and babies may thrive
The gypsies took this one and kept it alive
They fed it and raised it until it was five
But you can't tie a little girl down
And so one day she ran away
In the middle of Colchester town

> A baby's like rabies
> A devil well disguised
> Hateful, ungrateful
> She did a midnight flit, sir
> If she ends up in the shit, sir
> I wouldn't be a bit surprised

The Company disperse and there is a crossfade to:

SCENE 4

Colchester

Mayor enters on stilts holding the five-year-old Moll by the hand

Mayor What's this? A stray? A ragamuffin, rascal, a thing revolting and scabrous. Who owns this thing? Come on, come on. Ain't you got no home to go to? Oh dear me, no home. Well, what we do with strays is round 'em up and shut 'em up. We can't have the likes of you roaming the streets of Colchester providing an eyesore and a terror to the good citizens what have elected me as their Lord Mayor. It's the poorhouse for you. Nurse!

Nurse enters, also on stilts, carrying a ledger, pen and inkwell

I mean to keep an eye on you. Nurse, take this thing, humanize it, clean it up, make it presentable and inculcate it with some manners. Book.

Nurse hands Mayor the ledger and pen, and holds the inkwell

Item. One child. Sex?
Nurse It's a girl.
Mayor Female. Age?
Nurse About five.
Mayor Five years of age. Name?
Nurse Got a name, have you, darling?

Moll produces the note left by her mother

Mayor Oh, got it in writing have we? (*Reading*) "Look after my baby. Elizabeth Wright." (*Writing*) Elizabeth Wright. (*He shuts the book*) Right, nothing right about you so far, is there? Well, let's see if we can't get it right in future, eh?

Nurse takes Moll off

(*Aside*) And so it is, ladies and gentlemen, until it is time for the child to be sent out into the world to earn her keep. Nurse!

Nurse returns with Moll, now eight

(*Opening the book*) The record says this child is eight. Why isn't she working?

Nurse I told her, "We all have to work, child, so you'll have to go." But crying and weeping and clinging to me she was.

Moll (*weeping and clinging to Nurse*) Please, please, Nursie. Don't want to go in service. Do dirty work, be dog's thingie, cleaning an' peeling potatoes, an' getting all greasy an' smelly an' horrible.

Mayor Stop feeding her.

Nurse And telling her she loved me and didn't want to leave me.

Moll Love you, love you, Nursie. Don't send me away, please.

Mayor There's no money.

Nurse They won't work you too hard to start off.

Moll They will, they will. An' they'll beat me, The maids'll hit me black and blue, get me to scrub I'll have to scrub an' scrub all the floors. Am only little girl.

Mayor You've got to learn that your place in life is to be a servant.

Nurse The sooner you get started, the better.

Moll Don't want to be no servant.

Nurse Don't know what else you'll think you'll be. A gentlewoman, I suppose.

Moll Nursie, Nursie, yes.

Mayor What?

Nurse A gentlewoman.

Mayor (*laughing*) A ragamuffin turned gentlewoman.

Moll Want to be like that gentlewoman Nursie knows. She sits in the window an' mends the lace an' washes the ladies' caps, she does an' all. She got her own living.

Nurse Hush, child! That is a whore with two poor bastards to feed.

Moll Whore?

Mayor A gentlewoman! Wait till I tell the wife.

Moll Please, please, kind Nursie, be good an' work an' sew an' get money.

Nurse She does make a neat stitch. And she does go at it. Fair glutton for hard work, she is. She might get enough sewing to earn her keep.

Mayor She's neat, you say? The wife's looking for a little seamstress. She likes to combine charity with practicality. You can keep her. I'll tell the wife. (*He shuts the book*)

Nurse and Moll exit

And so it is that Bess is taken up by some of the better-class wives of
Colchester. She lives with the Nurse for the next four years. Until the old
woman dies ...

Moll enters, now twelve

Well, miss, the citizens of Colchester have done what they can for you; now
you're twelve you'll have to fend for yourself.

Moll Sir, my old nurse kept my savings for me.

Mayor So?

Moll Her daughter's taken everything.

Mayor I can't help that. I told you, be off with you, we can't keep you any
longer. You'll have to make your own way.

Moll No home, no nurse, no money. I can only pray like my nurse taught me.
(*She kneels and sings*)

Song 4: Moll's Prayer

The gypsies once told me you live on a mountain
A beautiful mountain, all rocky and wild
And Nurse used to say that a prayer is an arrow
And none flies as fast as the prayer of a child

But a mountain is tall and a voice is so small ...
Can a prayer lose its way? I suppose that it could
If I should lose mine, then how far might I fall?
So arrow fly true, for I want to be good

I've wandered the streets and I've searched for my mother
In each gentle face that I pass on the way
And God make me brave so I'll go on believing
Perhaps if I'm good, then I'll find her one day

And somehow I know, though she left long ago
She'll be tender and kind as a real mother should
And we'll both be so happy ... Oh, let it be so!
I'm trying so hard, and I want to be good

So if you can hear me, I beg you be near me
The world is so wicked, but God make me good

There is a crossfade to:

SCENE 5

Lady Constable's home

Lady Constable and her daughter Corrinder enter

Lady Constable Corrinder, we are going to have to find a new gel to do our sewing. The poorhouse nurse has died, so that child has gone.
Corrinder Gone? Has she died too, Mama?
Lady Constable No, no; but the poorhouse guardians won't keep her now the nurse is dead.
Corrinder But I liked her, Mama.
Lady Constable Dear little thing, wasn't she.
Corrinder She was my best friend.
Lady Constable Truth is beauty, child. No need to let sentiment overrule it. She was only a maid.
Corrinder Mama, you know you promised me a pony? Well couldn't I have a maid instead?
Lady Constable Corrinder, at moments like this I am proud to be your mama.

Corrinder exits

(*Aside*) And so it was that I became Betsy's fairy godmother, and by the time she was fifteen we looked upon her almost as part of the furniture — the family, I mean.

Corrinder returns, tugging Moll along excitedly

Corrinder Mama, Mama, look. Betsy is so clever. She can sing nearly as well as I can, and dance, and I'm sure she could play the spinet if only she had one to play. And, and, and she can speak better French than me — really! because I hate to roll my Rs and she doesn't mind what faces she pulls. Can she be in our picture, please?
Lady Constable In our family portrait?
Corrinder She can sit at my feet.
Lady Constable Well, you would look grand. There aren't many gels who are painted with their own maids. (*She claps her hands*)

Artist, Robert and Cyril enter and the portrait materializes. Robert is holding a brace of pheasants. The family poses

The Constable family portrait will be a picture to remember. Concentrate. Heads up, shoulders back, stomachs in, remember which is your best profile.

Robert My arm aches.

Lady Constable (*aside*) My younger son, Robert. (*To Robert*) Smile, Robert, let no-one know the agony of creation.

Robert And they stink.

Lady Constable Suffer, my son. We are all suffering.

Cyril (*gazing at Moll*) I'm not. I could stay like this forever, Mama.

Lady Constable Betsy ... sit!

Song 5: Portrait Song

Artist	Chin up!
Family	Chin up, chin up, chin up!
Artist	Chest in!
Family	Chest in, chest in, chest in!
Lady Constable	Don't sag!
Family	Don't sag, don't sag, don't sag!
Lady Constable	Don't grin!
Family	Don't grin!
Lady Constable	Corrinder!
Cyril	How her eyes do shine!
	How can a look enthral so!
	Virgin flesh, so young and fresh
	What more could an artist need, sir?
	I must make her mine
	For I am an artist also
	Of pleasures lush and lovers' toil
	Cheeks that flush and limbs that coil
	To dip the brush in sweeter oil
	A masterpiece indeed, sir
	So innocent and chaste
	Pretty little waist
	Never been embraced
	And never had a taste of Cupid's fire
	Oh, what endless rapture
	Would echo in my heart
	If I could but capture
	Betsy with my art
	The burning colours of desire

Lady Constable (*aside*) My elder son, Cyril. (*To Cyril*) How very noble and
   indeed Roman you look, Cyril.
Cyril Corrinder must take the credit. It was an inspired idea to have Betsy
   in our picture.
Corrinder Oh, do you think so?
Cyril We shall be like the Holy Family attended by our own seraph. Betsy
   is an angel, and when she blows her trumpet we shall all float away on a
   pink cloud.
Lady Constable Don't be so foolishly sacrilegious, Cyril.
Corrinder He is a fool. I don't want her spoiled.
Robert But he's right for once.

Lady Constable	(*singing*) Back straight!
Family	Back straight, back straight, back straight!
Lady Constable	Less gut!
Family	Less gut, less gut, less gut!
Lady Constable	More lift!
Family	More lift, more lift, more lift!
Artist	Mouth shut!
Family	Mouth shut!
Artist	(*to Lady Constable; singing*) Mouth shut!

Lady Constable slowly closes her mouth

Robert   A fever dims my eyes
                    And Betsy alone can cure it
                    Let Mother cry, I swear that my
                    Resolve will never falter

                    To lose so rare a prize
                    Oh, how could a man endure it?
                    With such fair game, then come what may
                    The hunter's aim should never stray
                    To catch and tame his dainty prey
                    And lead her to the altar

                    She's a commoner it's true
                    And she hasn't got a sou
                    But it's Betsy I shall woo
                    For the treasure I pursue is its own delight

                    I will be the hound and

> She will be the hare!
> Think of all the boundless
> Pleasures we will share
> The languid pleasures of the night ——

Lady Constable (*interrupting; speaking*) Robert!
Robert Yes, Mama?

Lady Constable (*singing*) Chin up!
Family Chin up, chin up, chin up!
Lady Constable Chin up!

Artist (*speaking*) Relax!
Lady Constable Oh, Betsy dear, go and fetch the bon-bons.
Robert The whole town is talking of her. They say she deserves a rich husband.
Lady Constable A rich husband! The gel is a maid.
Robert Sorry, Mother, but it's the truth.
Lady Constable Truth is beauty child, and like beauty it is often irrelevant. The market is against our sex just now, and if a young woman has beauty, birth, breeding, wit, sense and manners, modesty, and all to an extreme, and yet she does not have money, then she is a nobody. Nothing but money recommends a woman.
Robert Gibberish.
Corrinder I beg your pardon?
Robert Pure gibberish and unpardonable parrot rot! No-one could look at Betsy and think of money. She has the power to transform our dreary, mercenary lives. And pretty maids can expect to be married before their plain mistresses.
Corrinder Plain?
Robert If the cap fits.
Corrinder Take that back.
Robert It does, it does!
Lady Constable Children! Children!
Corrinder (*screaming with frustration*) Oo! Oo!
Lady Constable Corrinder!
Corrinder Make him take it back! It's not fair! I hate him. I hate ... (*She breaks into sobs*)
Lady Constable Corrinder, don't be so wastefully emotional! Think of your toilet. We cannot have our family portrait ruined by a blotchy face. Betsy, run and fetch your mistress her face powder and some rouge.

Moll and Artist exit

There is a crossfade to:

SCENE 6

Song 6: The Seduction

Moll I am sad when they quarrel over me. Still, it is wondrous to be so praised.

A musical vamp underscores Moll as she goes about her maidly chores in the form of a choreographed ballet. Throughout, members of the family appear, order her around and disappear

Moll   Mend the stockings and the gowns and clean the shoes and
      fetch the food and drink and make the beds
     Run her bath and get her gloves and do her hair and sew
      the hem she trod on yesterday
     Light the fires and air the room and feed the cockatoo, that
      wretched cockatoo that pecks my hand
     And scrub the floor and wash the clothes and empty out
      the slops and sometimes sit and dream of love

Lady Constable enters and catches Moll day-dreaming

Lady Constable (*severely*) Remember well
     A maid's a maid
     And only made to serve
     And maids who put on maiden's airs
     Will get what they deserve

Moll   Mend the stockings and the gowns and clean the shoes and
      fetch the food and drink and make the beds
     Run her bath and get her gloves and do her hair and sew
      the hem she trod on yesterday

Lady Constable Remember well
     A maid's a maid
     And only made to serve
     And maids who put on maiden's airs
     Will get what they deserve

Lady Constable leaves

Moll continues whistling her tune

Cyril enters

Cyril Look at her. She is an angel. But will she answer my prayers?

He startles her

Betsy!
Moll What is it?
Cyril Oh Betsy, may I lie in your lap?
Moll Master Cyril?
Cyril I mean my *head* in your lap. Did you think I meant country matters?
Moll I don't understand.
Cyril You silly thing. It's Shakespeare. Poetry.
Moll Oh.
Cyril I can be a poet too, you know.

> (*Singing*) Come with me, maid!
> Our meeting's clandestine
> Yet still we may rest in
> The arbour of love
>
> Don't be afraid
> The angels delight in
> Two souls that unite in
> The harbours of love
>
> Some leafy glade
> Will be our bower
> Seize but the hour
> And it's ours for eternity
> Never to fade
> But stay as a token
> Of vows left unspoken
> Yet ever obeyed

(*Speaking*) Betsy, I love you. There.
Moll Now you are teasing me.
Cyril No, no, I'm in deadly earnest. Never been more serious. I tried to weave

a poem round your name ... but I couldn't. Words deserted me. I just had to blurt it out. Forgive me, Betsy.

Moll There's nothing to forgive.

Cyril Oh but there is, there is. I should never have embarrassed you by telling you of my love. I do love you, you know.

Moll Please.

Cyril (*stifling a sob*) I'm sorry, Betsy.

Moll (*aside*) No man has ever told me he loves me before. It makes me feel ... giddy. My stomach is full of goldfish. My head is full of pink and white clouds. I want to hear him say it again.

Cyril exits

Moll begins day-dreaming again, then pulls herself together and starts to sweep

> (*To herself; singing*) Remember well
> A maid's a maid
> And only made to serve
> And maids who put on maiden's airs
> Will get what they deserve

There are a few bars of vamp

Robert enters and admires her

Robert   Enchanting maid!
                  Was ever maid
                  By heaven made so fine?
                  I've made a vow I'll never rest
                  Until I've made her mine

Moll   And so I'll mend the stockings and the gowns and clean
                      the shoes and fetch the food and drink and make the beds
                  Run her bath and get her gloves and do her hair and sew
                      the hem she trod on yesterday

Robert   (*more lyrically*)
                  Enchanting maid!
                  Was ever maid
                  By heaven made so fine?
                  I've made a vow I'll never rest
                  Until I've made her mine

Moll   (*also more lyrically, as she dreams of Cyril*)
                            Remember well
                            A maid's a maid
                            And only made to serve
                            And maids who put on maiden's airs
                            Will get what they deserve

Cyril enters

Cyril Robert, Mama wants you to apologize to Corrinder.

Robert exits

Cyril approaches Moll and kisses her

How can I make you believe I love you? (*He produces a bag of gold*) Five
gold guineas.
Moll What?
Cyril I want to give you a present. It's not much. Just something to show that
I mean it. Please take them.

Molls draws back

Please. (*He puts the bag into her hand*)
Moll I have never seen gold before. It's beautiful. It shines like the sun.
Cyril Agh! This is torment! How can you be so cruel, Betsy?
Moll Cruel? Torment?
Cyril I will run stark, staring mad for love of you, I swear it. Oh, say you care
for me. Just a little.
Moll I ... dear Cyril, I don't know.
Cyril Trust me. Trust me, I adore you.
Moll Trust you? (*She sings*)

                            Sir, I am a maid
                            And maids often stray with
                            A man who makes play with
                            The lies of the world

                            But, once she has strayed
                            A maid's brought to ruin
                            A whore through and through in
                            The eyes of the world

> Once she's betrayed
> There's no redress
> So, sir, I confess
> I'd say yes in a trice
> But the price must be paid
> If love is requited
> Then troths must be plighted
> And words must be weighed

Corrinder (*off*) Betsy!

Corrinder bustles in as Cyril exits hastily

> Did you mend the stockings and the gowns and clean the
>   shoes and fetch the food and drink and make the beds?
> And did you run my bath and get my gloves? And here's
>   another hem I must have trod on yesterday

During the following, Lady Constable enters and overhears Corrinder

> (*To the audience*) How nice to have
> A trusty maid
> To carry, fetch and send.
> But, better still, I think at last
> I might have made a friend.

Moll   Yes, I did the stockings and the gowns and cleaned the
>   shoes and fetched the food and drink and made the beds
> And ran the bath and got the gloves, and not another hem
>   I sewed one only yesterday ——

Lady Constable (*to Corrinder*) Remember well
> A maid's a maid
> And only made to serve
> And maids who put on maiden's airs
> Will get what they deserve

Moll   —I've lit the fire and aired the room and fed the wretched
>   cockatoo, how I hate cockatoos
> And scrubbed the floor and washed the clothes and
>   emptied out the contents of my lady's chamber pot——

Robert enters

*Moll continues singing alone as she advances towards the front of the stage,
while Corrinder and Lady Constable back off to form an arc upstage with
Robert*

    Cyril enters from one side and slowly moves towards Moll

> — And I run and think of him, and fetch and think of him
> and sweat and think of him, and even though I know
> I should be strong, how can I help but think of him, and
> who can blame me if I dream of love?

*Lady Constable, Corrinder and Robert softly sing the following as a round,
initially with Moll singing a counter-melody, then they continue softly
underneath the dialogue between Cyril and Moll*

Corrinder	Mend the stockings and the gowns and clean the shoes and fetch the food and drink and make the beds ——
Robert	Enchanting maid! Was ever maid so fine? I swear I'll never rest until I've made her mine ——
Lady Constable	Remember well: a maid is just a maid, and maids who put on airs will get what they deserve ——
Moll	I dream of love ——

Moll's reverie is again interrupted by Cyril

Cyril Dear Betsy, I want to marry you when I can. That is, when my pater dies and I come into my inheritance.
Moll Do you?
Cyril And you will marry me, won't you?
Moll Oh, yes!
Cyril You will? I've got this for you. (*He produces a bag*) It's only more gold, I'm afraid. (*Aside*) Got to leave her. I want so ... I am so ... Damn it! I love her and I don't want to hurt her. She believes I'm going to marry her, and I believe it too, God knows I do. I can't wait that long. (*To Moll*) Betsy, I'm not asking for anything. It's just that I am in such pain. I don't want pity. I want ... perhaps it would afford me some relief to hold your hand. To touch you. Touching is merely the physical expression of my love. Believe me, all I ask for if the union of our minds ——
Moll Union. It sounds so wonderful.
Cyril — and bodies.

Moll A solemn union.

Cyril   (*aside; singing*) So easily swayed!
                             Some tender words tendered
                             Her hymen's surrendered
                             An excellent trade!

                             For promises made
                             Are made for breaking
                             When maids are for taking
                             In love's masquerade
Moll   Would you marry a maid?
Cyril   Fair maid, I will!
                             But first let's fulfil this sweet promise of paradise
Moll   Our hearts will be filled with a lifetime of paradise
Cyril   Come with me, maid
                             And we shall savour
                             The joy of love's favour
                             So pray do not waver
                             But come, come, come, come lie with me, maid

Corrinder   Mend the stockings and the gowns and clean the shoes and
                             fetch the food and drink and make the beds ——
Robert   Enchanting maid! Was ever maid so fine? I swear I'll
                             never rest until I've made her mine ——
Lady Constable   Remember well: a maid is just a maid, and maids who put
                             on airs will get what they deserve ——

Corrinder
Robert   } (*together*) Betsy!
Lady Constable

They exit

Moll and Cyril disappear. After a moment Cyril reappears

Cyril Oh, believe me Betsy, I'd ask you to marry me now, go down and beg
on my bended knees, but I can't at the moment because I haven't come into
my inheritance yet. But what is marriage, dear Betsy? A piece of paper! A
formality. It is what is in our hearts and minds that matters. Heaven knows
that all ready. (*Aside*) Ladies and gentlemen, sex as a blood sport. The thrill
of the chase. Run to earth. In for the kill. However, now our affair is

established, I'm surprising myself by continuing to enjoy it. Thoroughly! Though I am beginning to worry in a desultory fashion about the eventual outcome of it all. Dear Betsy sees a life of perpetual bliss spread out before us like some magical oriental carpet. Whereas I, who have no intention of wedding her, begin to consider what danger the poor child stands in should the affair be discovered. She's young and, although no longer a virgin, innocent. Besides, I'm excessively fond of her and have no wish to see her come to grief.

There is a crossfade to:

SCENE 7

Music

The rest of the family return and take their places for the portrait

Cyril Pwaugh! Those birds, brother!

Robert Yes, they're fairly well hung.

Cyril Aren't we all.

Lady Constable Boys. Present those profiles!

Robert Mama, I have a confession to make.

Lady Constable The church is the place for confession, Robert.

Robert I can't keep it for church. I am madly, passionately in love.

Lady Constable Not before lunch dear, please.

Robert But Mama, I've made up my mind, all I want is your permission to declare myself.

Lady Constable Robert, I will tell you when you are in love. It is a parent's duty to ensure their children love the right woman.

Robert But, that's it exactly! I love the Wright woman!

Lady Constable Robert, who exactly are you talking about.

Robert Betsy, Mama.

Lady Constable Oh, of course, Betsy Wright. Betsy?! The maid?

Moll No ... I ... no!

Lady Constable This is ghastly. Betsy, is this how you repay me? Robert, I am not having you marrying into the great unwashed. A maid is a maid. You'd do well to remember that, Betsy.

Robert It's not fair.

Lady Constable Indeed it isn't. I was so hoping that we could get this wretched portrait painted and now I find that I shall have to retire to my room with a headache. Come along, Corrinder.

Corrinder I shan't be requiring your services at the moment, Betsy.

Lady Constable and Corrinder exit

Moll What did she mean?

Robert Dear Betsy, let me speak to you.

Moll No, I can't.

Cyril A word of advice, brother. (*He takes Robert aside*)

Moll (*aside*) Robert? In love with me? What will Cyril think? He'll think I've
been a flirt. And I haven't, I haven't.

Robert exits

Cyril Well, Betsy my love, you seem to have had quite an effect on my dear
brother.

Moll Don't tease.

Cyril Poor man.

Moll It's nothing to do with me. I've done nothing to encourage him.

Cyril I know; but it makes things devilish difficult for us.

Moll You have to tell them about us, Cyril.

Cyril Yes, you saw how Mama reacted though.

Moll She was horrid.

Cyril I know, but it would have been ten times worse if it had been me. I mean
I'm the eldest. The son and heir.

Moll Dear Cyril, we will have to be very brave.

Cyril The disappointment might even kill her.

Moll Cyril?

Cyril My sweet?

Moll Do you love me?

Cyril You know I do. Haven't I proved it a thousand times, and even now ...
but it's because I love you I really think it would be best if you married
brother Robert.

Moll But I can't, I'm married already.

Cyril Who to?

Moll You! We have said it again and again. Husband and wife in everything
but name.

Cyril Yes, but that's the ticklish bit. We cannot be legally married for fear
Mama disinherits me, so ——

Moll I won't marry Robert!

Cyril I'm afraid you must, Betsy. And furthermore, you must erase from
your memory everything that has passed between us. I freely release you
from any promises you may have made to me, and I fully expect you to do
likewise.

Moll But we're married!

Cyril Pay attention, Betsy. I am going to have to work extremely hard to persuade Mama to allow this wedding and I expect your co-operation.
Moll I'll tell her.
Cyril And in that case you will be thrown out on the streets again and your reputation will be utterly ruined. And to make our separation easier to bear, if you are a good girl, I propose to give you a dowry of five hundred guineas.

The Chorus (including Robert) enter

Song 7: Her Love Made Her Rich

Chorus   Her love made her rich, but she traded too deeply
                  The future she banked on was only a dream
                  For now she can see that his credit was worthless
                  The promise he gave her he'll never redeem
                  The interest on sin is a few golden guineas
                  And gold may be bright but it's cold to the touch
                  Their bond was invalid, their books never tallied
                  He loved her a little, she loved him too much

                  She mortgaged her heart at too high a percentage
                  But now it's foreclosed all her prospects are bare
Moll   Examine our deeds once before you withdraw, love
                  Before you withdraw love and bank it elsewhere

Cyril Goodbye, Betsy.

During the following chorus, Moll and Robert are married

Chorus   The sum of his feeling was mere double-dealing
                  He squandered her birthright and plundered her trust
Moll   Now that, too, is lost, for I've learned to my cost
                  What seems to be priceless may only be dust
                  So, God grant your pardon if my heart should harden
                  If I cannot be good, then I'll be what I must

Robert (*aside*) Dear friends, sex as an integral part of holy matrimony. A private affair leading to the birth of children. (*He smiles*) In our case — two!
Moll (*aside*) I am living in a dream. In all respects I behave as Robert's wife but I feel nothing. How I come to have his children is almost a mystery to me. When I lie beside him I can only see the face of his brother. Dear God in heaven, why do you make me nightly commit adultery, incest and bigamy? When will you set me free?

Moll exits. Lady Constable enters with two babies

Lady Constable Sad to say our family portrait was never completed. We had just included the charming heiress who had become dear Cyril's bride when Robert fell ill and died. Poor Betsy is heartbroken. She finds his children a constant reproach, so I, for one, am not surprised that she is settling them on me and going to live in London.

There is a crossfade to:

SCENE 8

London

Music

Luke, Ralph and Henry lurk in various attitudes. Moll enters

Moll I am now in the best possible position a woman can be in. I am a rich widow, and in addition I have youth, beauty, wit and an appetite for pleasure.

Luke Sweet music, how shall we divert ourselves today? A trip to the Spring Gardens at Vauxhall?

Henry Dear lady, will you accompany me to Hyde Park, where we might hire a telescope and perhaps catch sight of a Royal personage?

Ralph Mrs Constable, can I tempt you to make a visit to my civet factory? I'm sure you'd find it fascinating.

Moll Life is one continual round of solicitations! It is like living in a masque at the opera ...

Song 8: The Masque

Luke   (*offering lace*) Dear heart, here's some lace that a queen
                    might prize
                  For a garter to place on your queenly thighs
                  But 'twould bite if too tight, and a fitting is fitting
                  So lift up your skirts and I'll take your size

Moll   Though, sir, your suggestion might tempt me to sin
                  I'm not a young virgin so easy to win ——

Luke   But virginity's queer
                  Once you lose it, my dear
                  You can still use the box that you kept it in

Ralph (*offering perfume*) Mrs Constable, may I beg you to accept this
sample of my finest perfume, produced from the musk glands of the civet
cat, at my aforementioned civet factory?

Moll Perfume, from cats?

Ralph	Oh, the gland of a civet is wondrous rare
	And a civet's activities fill the air
	I had planned to expand, but the backing was lacking
	Invest, and I'll make you a millionaire!
Moll	I thank you, good sir, for your kind guarantees
	But where are these glands, could you tell me, please?
Ralph	Do come and inspect 'em
	They're just by the rectum
	And if you behave you can have a squeeze!
Henry	(*referring to Luke*)
	If you follow this gent, then it's bed he'll propose
	(*referring to Ralph*)
	If you follow his scent you'll be led by the nose
	So I'll press my own suit with this plain, honest fruit
	(*He offers her an apple*)
	I'm a man of few words and no fancy prose
	My lace is the apron you'll wear when we're wed
	My scent is the perfume of newly-baked bread
	Don't mix with these dregs
	With their brains 'twixt their legs
	Bring my apple to chapel, take me instead!
Luke	No, no, take me instead
Ralph	No, no, take me instead ... take me, take me, Mrs Constable
Moll	(*silencing them all*)
	The choice is a hard one I have to confess
	My hand up a civet, or yours up my dress
	No, I think on reflection
	I've made my selection
	Security's best, sir, my answer
	My answer, my answer is ... yes

She gives Henry his apple back and they eat a piece each

   Luke, Ralph and Moll exit

Henry Ladies and gentlemen, sex at the corner shop, fair trading and no short measures. (*He munches on his apple*) Beauty of Bath, I'd say. Only problem is, with her extra money I've become extravagant. Imagining myself a man of property instead of a mere tradesman. She may have nothing against trade, but I have. So I've taken up card playing with the gentry, and now, three years later, here I am in prison on account of my gambling debts. All the money's gone. Hers as well as mine. I'd better write to her. Dear Wife, sorry about this letter but we're ruined. All I can say is, it was fun while it lasted. Upon consideration I think it would be best if we forgot we were ever married.

Moll enters with a letter

Henry ⎫ (*together; reading*)   You take anything and everything you can
Moll ⎭   pawn from the house and take it quick.
Moll It won't amount to much but it's the best I can do in the circumstances. If I can get out of this hole I'll flee to France and never return to England. So, farewell, dear wife that was. Henry.
Henry PS Kiss the mole on your right breast for me. (*He tosses Moll the apple core*) Well, she was a good-looking woman, know what I mean?

There is a crossfade to:

SCENE 9

The Mint

Gambler, Drunkard and Fornicator enter

Moll Since my husband has left bills all over the city I am changing my name to Moll Flanders and I am going to live in The Mint. The Mint is an area comprising two or three mean, foul-smelling streets where debtors and degenerates are protected from prosecution providing they do not venture beyond its boundaries. It is a hellish place full of ——

Song 9: The Mint

Gambler	Misery
Drunkard	Desolation
Fornicator	And despair
All	When your debts leave you skint
	You end up in the Mint

	With the scoundrels, cut-throats, footpads, whores and knaves
Gambler	We're the lowest of the low
Drunkard	Down as far as we can go
Fornicator	Till they lower us down into our graves
Gambler ⎫	
Drunkard ⎭	Into our graves
Gambler	I gamble ... I'm always at the table
Drunkard	I drink ... I'm often under the table
Fornicator	I fornicate ... on the table, under the table, I'm not choosy really
Gambler	Well, a gambler likes to win
Drunkard	And a drunkard likes his gin
Fornicator	And a man like me likes anything that moves!
Gambler	But my horse came down with gout
Drunkard	And my liver's up the spout
Fornicator	And my only willing partners now have hooves

Moll I have the greatest difficulty in avoiding the company of such men. I have found they take pleasure in paying for supper with a lady, even if that very day their wives have been begging them to provide a crust to feed their own children.

Lucie enters

Imagine my joy at meeting Lucie, a young widow, who feels as I do about our neighbours.

Lucie We are lonely widows.

Moll (*aside*) Her husband was captain of a ship, lost at sea with all their fortune. And I had "lost" mine ... to be sociable.

Lucie We are a pathetic sight!

Moll Dear Lucie, what has happened to us is a miscarriage of natural justice. It is not our fault we are surrounded by ——

Gambler	Misery
Drunkard	Desolation
Fornicator	And despair!

During the following, Lucie receives a letter

All	When your debts leave you skint
	And you wind up in the Mint
	You know you've reached the bottom of the heap!
	When you're breaking bread with scum

> There's a simple rule of thumb
> You're no better than the company you keep

Gambler, Drunkard and Fornicator exit

Lucie (*referring to the letter*) Moll! Deliverance! All my husband's fortune was not lost with him. I still have money!

Moll What luck for you.

Lucie And you, Moll. Come with me. I aim to find myself another husband. Let's to the seaside. I fancy another sailor! Come, what do you say? A pair of sailors!

Moll A pair of sailors!

They exit

There is a crossfade to:

Scene 10

A quayside public house and its environs

Two sailors, Abe and Jerry, are drinking, with a publican and barmaid on hand

Song 10: A Sailor's Life

Jerry } **Abe**	The life of a sailor ain't grand, boys When you're six months away from land, boys
Jerry	And frustration increases, your only release is hard work Or the palm of your hand, boys
Both	It's not very pleasant, it's true!
Jerry	But then what's a poor sailor to do?
Both	And ashore what's even worse is The feel of your empty purses
Jerry	But why both with empty curses? If he marries the right sort of girl
Both	A sailor can live like an earl!
	So we'll sink a schooner of porter And wink at some gentleman's daughter
Abe	And then at last we'll ride our mast Between the wind and the water

| **Jerry** | A woman will keep you warm |
| **Barmaid** | And it's any old port in a storm |

Abe ⎫	But poke 'em though we may, mates
Jerry ⎭	They'll never be more than playmates
	If they can't pay their way, mates
	For we'll take any woman to bed
	But it's only the wealthy we'll wed

The music continues

Abe Home at last.

Jerry I'm a tobacco planter — as British as a bulldog, but bred in the colonies. This is my first time home. What's it like?

Publican Small, wet and smells of cowshit.

Jerry But are the natives friendly?

Publican Not so you'd notice. They don't think much of tobacco planters, same as they don't think much of sailors.

Jerry Why?

Abe We're beneath them. We risk our lives to make them wealthy and they laugh at the way we talk and call us uncouth. Well I intend to rob a piece of their complacency and get me a rich wife before I set sail again. She can buy me a new ship. She'll have to, the old one's past repairing.

Jerry A rich wife with a fine dowry — that's what I'm after too.

Abe Ten guineas I fetch up with one before you get a sniff.

Jerry Done.

They shake hands

   Moll and Lucie enter

Abe An argosy to larboard.

Jerry Two.

Abe Man the guns.

Lucie Ahem. Sailors.

Abe Ma'am.

Jerry Ma'am.

Instrumental — Lucie and Abe pair off and stroll

   Moll and Jerry pair off and exit

Lucie I find the sea front so stimulating, so close to the elements! And you

have actually been out there? On the seas. Tempting providence! Oh you
must be so brave.

Abe If you say so, ma'am.

Lucie I find the wild ocean so compelling. It puts me in mind of mermaids
and lost treasure and piratical young men who sweep one off one's feet.

Abe Allow me, ma'am. (*He picks her up*)

Lucie How masterful! But first I must enquire as to your fortune. I do hope
you are one of those pirates who are simply dripping with precious stones.

Abe Ma'am, I am a pirate proud to sail beneath one flag; the flag of honour.

Lucie But honour can make a hard bed for a bride to lie in. A little money
might serve as a bolster. You sir, have questioned me in great detail about
my fortune.

Abe Would you have me pursue an empty vessel?

Lucie Would you have me surrender to a rowing boat?

Abe A rowing boat? You seem to forget, ma'am, that I am a man, and you
are a mere woman. In plain terms, you must take my word on such matters
or lose me altogether. Good-day, ma'am.

The music stops

Lucie Oh!

Jerry and Moll enter

Jerry No fortune?

Moll Save my looks, my accomplishments, which are many, and my
pleasing temperament. I would make you an excellent wife.

Jerry You lack the one quality that would endear you to me. Gold. Farewell.
(*To Abe*) Shall we go fish in more abundant waters?

Abe Ay, for there's only minnows here!

Abe and Jerry exit

The introduction to Song 11 starts

Moll They would marry pigs if pigs had golden snouts. Without a dowry I
shall never get a husband. It is the dread of every woman to be without a
husband and without the means of getting one. And a single woman has the
same value in society as a single shoe in a wardrobe.

Lucie (*weeping*) He's gone. My one and only true love; he's gone.

Moll True? Since when was any man true?

Song 11: Lap-dogs

A man is like a lap-dog, so charming when he begs
But all he really wants to do is lie between our legs
He'll promise to be faithful, and never think to stray
But he'll sniff at any bitch on heat he passes on his way
It's a topsy-turvy world, my friend, as any fool can see
When you and I are chained for life, and all the dogs run free

Moll But we are not to be bested by lap-dogs. Lucie, you're sure you want him?
Lucie Oh, I shall die unless I marry him.
Moll Well, suppose you ran a shop ——
Lucie But I'm not going to run a shop! Are you mad? I hate tradespeople!
Moll Listen, Lucie, suppose you ran a bank, and a customer came in asking
  for credit. Would you give it to him?
Lucie That would depend upon his reputation.
Moll And if it were bad, what would you call him?
Lucie Uncreditworthy.
Moll Precisely. So inform the world he refused to tell you the size of his
  fortune because he hasn't got one. No-one will contemplate marrying him then.
Lucie And he will hate me.
Moll Not when he finds he can't get a wife elsewhere. He'll swallow his
  damned honour and come back to you. In any case, I'll do it for you. (*She
  sings*)

Her wedding's off — a good thing too! — for, if he ups
  and dies
He wouldn't have a penny piece to place upon his eyes
The sweets he bought were mouldy, her engagement ring
  was paste
His clothes are torn or else in pawn, his credit is disgraced
So shun this fine young buccaneer, whatever else you do
Himself he's ruined on his own, don't let him ruin you!

Lucie Now it's my turn.
Moll What?

Lucie

My friend's as rich as Croesus, with fine plate on every shelf
But she's vowed she'll only wed a man who loves her for
  herself
So she keeps her wealth a secret from the fortune-hunting
  bores

But if you were to marry her a fortune would be yours
So take my tip and woo her well, a task you won't regret
Convince her that you love her and you'll be a rich man yet

Abe and Jerry enter

Abe I can't understand it. No-one will marry me.
Jerry Dear lady, at last I've found you again.
Lucie (*to Abe*) Hallo-o.
Moll But you know I have no money.
Abe Look, about my fortune ——
Jerry I don't care about the money. I'll follow my heart ——
Moll (*aside*) To cut a long story short, several moonlit walks, a multitude of
   sweaty hand-holding and several gross of heart-rending sighs later ——

Abe   } (*together*) Will you marry us?
Jerry

Moll   } (*together*) Yes, we will.
Lucie

Abe   ⎫   (*Singing*) We took her tip and wooed them well
Jerry ⎭   A task we don't regret
                     We convinced them that we love them and
                     We'll both be rich men

Moll   ⎱   They think they're rich men
Lucie ⎰   But they're not rich men yet

Abe   ⎱   We'll both be rich men yet!
Jerry ⎰

Jerry Ladies and gentlemen, sex in return for the expectation of plenty. My
   dear, I thought we'd take a house in London for the season.
Moll Won't that be rather expensive?
Jerry Leave it to me. But now that we are married, I think I should take care
   of our joint fortunes.
Moll I agree.
Jerry You do?
Moll Of course.
Jerry Well what have you got for me?
Moll Nothing. You know that.
Jerry But, she said ——
Moll You shouldn't listen to rumour where love is concerned, my dear.
   Follow your heart.

Jerry But how else can we afford to live in this damned expensive hole?
Moll On your money?
Jerry What I've got might keep us in Virginia, but that's out of the question
   for a fine lady like yourself.
Moll But I'm not a fine lady, Jerry; I'm a tobacco planter's wife.
Jerry Virginia it is, then.

There is a crossfade to:

SCENE 11

Moll and Jerry are sailing to Virginia

Song 12: Sailing to Virginia

Moll ⎫
Jerry ⎭
                     Now destiny has entwined us
                     We're leaving our troubles behind us
                     So it's past the Azores
                     To Virginia's shores
                     Where nothing will ever remind us
                     Of the creditors at the door
                     And we'll never come back any more

                     A new life we'll begin there
                     And a fortune we will win there
Jerry   For everybody that's been there
                     Says the New World is dripping with gold
Moll   Which is more than you'd say of the Old

Both   We're sailing to Virginia
                     We're sailing to Virginia
                     We're sailing to Virginia, Virginia ...

They land

There is a crossfade to:

SCENE 12

Virginia

Elizabeth greets them and gently pulls them apart. Obviously, Moll and Elizabeth do not recognize each other

Elizabeth Welcome home, son.
Jerry Mother.

They embrace

Moll Virginia. America. The New World. Land of enterprise!
Jerry Mother, this is my wife; Moll, this is my mother.
Elizabeth Oh, what a beautiful woman.

They embrace

Jerry (*aside*) My mother and my wife are instant friends. It seems to me that I have all life's riches. I can't imagine being happier. And then our children are born, and I am.
Elizabeth (*aside*) I'm like the morning glory. The days pass so sweetly I never want to shut my petals. At last I have a friend, another woman to sit with in the evenings, to gossip and chatter and giggle with. (*To Moll*) He bought me you know. My husband. We often joked about it later, but he did. When we arrived to serve out our sentence, I was the one he chose.
Moll And did he come here as a convict — your husband?
Elizabeth Yes, we were all convicts once. Except Jerry, of course, he's second generation. But his father was very respectable by the time I met him. He'd served his time, worked hard and bought his own bit of land. That bit led to another, and another bit, his land accumulated. Everything accumulates out here. Everything seems possible. There's space, and there's light, and there's enough food to go round if you work for it and ... bit different from London, eh?
Moll Yes. Do you ever miss it?
Elizabeth No. This is my home. This is where I belong. I don't ever want to go back. Too many bad memories. That court, prison, the fear of the gallows and ... all the rest of it.
Moll The gallows?
Elizabeth Oh yes, I was sentenced to death, for stealing a roll of cloth.
Moll How did you escape?
Elizabeth Escape? No you couldn't escape, even the windows were in the bleeding ceiling. In Newgate, a man got me with child ... they couldn't hang you if you were pregnant, you see ... I've lived with the guilt ever since.
Moll But you had no choice, what else could you do?
Elizabeth I could have taken her with me, but I thought ... I don't know ...

that she'd have a better chance for a decent life in England than she would
sailing off to the ends of the earth in a convict ship. May God forgive me.
She was a pretty little thing. All I left her was a note.

Moll Can you remember what you wrote?

Elizabeth }
Moll   } (*together*) Look after my baby. Elizabeth Wright.

Elizabeth How did you know that that was my name before I was married?

*The music freezes the moment. The Lights change to suggest a move forward
in time to the evening. The scene dissolves to:*

SCENE 13

Song 13: Never Look Back (Finale)

Moll   I know I was happy but, truth to tell
                    I knew that my luck couldn't last
                    Any fool can escape from a prison cell
                    But no-one escapes from the past

                    You gave up your child, and that child was me
                    My children in turn I must quit
                    To bequeath them this shame in society
                    Is one sin I'll never commit

                    But I've still sinned so deeply, dear Mother
                    And the thought of it fills me with dread
                    What words can I say to my brother
                    Now incest has blighted our bed?

Elizabeth   Oh, Lord, how my crimes have come back to me
                    The circle has turned to its start
                    To lose you but once was like agony
                    Twice, though, will tear me apart!

*During the following, Jerry enters unseen by the two women and overhears
them*

Moll   I vowed as a child I would look for you
                    And see how God answers my prayer!
                    But we all have to pay for the things we do
                    Though the price may be too hard to bear

	So I beg you don't cry for me, Mother

So I beg you don't cry for me, Mother
For your tears cut as sharp as a knife
Just say what I was to my brother
His bride, yes, but never his wife

Elizabeth　What have I done?
Oh, how was I to know?
My daughter!

Jerry　Moll, is this true?
That you're leaving?
Say it's not true!
If you leave me, it will kill me!
Oh, Moll, I love you!

Moll　My love, kiss our children and hold them close
To leave you hurts more than you'll know
Our marriage was cursed but our love was true
Though all of my life I'll remember you
There's only one thing now that's left to do
To pack my belongings and go!

Jerry　No!
I beg you!
You will drive me to madness!
If you leave it will kill me!
Moll, I beg you, don't go!

Elizabeth　I should have died in that prison!
What will become of us now?
You will drive him to madness!
If you leave it will kill him!
Moll, I beg you, don't go!

Moll Mother, I must go at once, but I need help; money, a cargo of tobacco, anything to save me starving in England.
Jerry No, Moll!
Moll I must leave to protect all our reputations, dear Jerry.
Jerry But no-one need ever know!
Moll Besides, I have no legal standing as your wife. You could cast me off at any time. There is no security here for me any more.

Jerry grabs her

  Brother ——
Jerry No, not brother — husband!
Moll Don't, Jerry!
Jerry My love!
Moll How can you?

Moll stands frozen

Elizabeth Son, Moll is right. You will turn her affection to hate. What we
  have done is a sin, a sin against God.
Jerry Then there is no God!

He rushes off. The Company enter

*Moll and Elizabeth cling to each other as the Company move towards the
audience. Moll backs away upstage. She gets lost among the crowd, leaving
Elizabeth downstage waving to her*

Company	The course is set fair and the tide is high
	The breakers are pounding the shore
	All sailors and sweethearts must say goodbye
	It's time to weigh anchor once more
	And the winds, how they blow ever shriller!
	And the waves, how they rise and descend!
	But whose is the hand on the tiller?
	Who can say when their journey will end?
Moll	God, can this be?
	Oh, my mother, how can this be?
	First to find you
	Then to lose you again forever!
Company	So never look back on the past, my friends!
	The storm is too strong in the sail!
	Remorse and regret make a bitter brew
	Who knows where your destiny's taking you?
	Perhaps just a little bit closer to
	The gallows at Newgate Gaol

CURTAIN

ACT II

The pump room at Bath

Music

Society men and women promenade on the stage

Sycophant Have you taken the waters today, your lordship?

Lord Indeed I have, sir, and feel much the better for it.

Sycophant Ah, they say no waters on earth have the restorative powers of those of Bath.

Lord And they say right, sir. " 'Pon my soul, there's no place like Bath ..."

Woman Men take the waters to cleanse the inner man, and a mistress to free him from physical desire. With the result that it is no good looking for a husband in Bath, nor a wife for that matter either. It is all a matter of lusting for whatever you fancy.

They stroll off

Song 14: Bath Promenade

Company   If dropsy or ague should happen to plague you
A person of substance knows where to convene
Go beat out a path to the pump room at Bath
You may not be cured, but at least you'll be seen

Take tea with a duke in a powdered peruke
See a duchess on crutches if such is your sport
But, great though they are, undressed in a spa
They look much the same as the ordinary sort

Moll is revealed, surrounded by male admirers

Moll (*aside*) My journey back to England turned into a nightmare. We sailed into horrific storms. Our ship was near destroyed and my cargo of tobacco

completely ruined. I thought my last moment had come. It may still come.
I've written to my mother for help, and if she doesn't send that soon I face
starvation and certain death. I've come to Bath to wait. To pass the time I
go out and about in society.

Company	All history teaches there's no need for leeches
	For Bath's been the place since the heyday of Rome
	Your goitre or gout will be cured, there's no doubt
Moll	But, if you have pox, won't you please stay at home!
	Each day you may gaze on a secret liaison
	Between say a prince and some fair *ingénue*
	While odours of sulphur will clear out your skull for
	The secret liaisons that wait there for you

We see Biggins preparing for his bath

Biggins I am a poor invalid, sick in mind and body, and come to Bath to seek
relief in its health-giving springs. I had hoped to see Mrs Flanders, a most
charming widow whom I met yesterday, but it seems that even that small
comfort is to be denied me. Oh, I am a most wretched man.

> (*Singing*) My wife is insane, my children are foul
> These waters are poison for all I can tell
> There's bile on my brain and a flux in my bowel
> And Bath smells as bad as the gateway to Hell!

Moll	Oh, come now, my friend, see it through to the end
	There's many a slip 'twixt the cup and the lip
Biggins	(*drinking*) Well, since you're so nice, I shall take your advice
	And if you'll support me I'll go for a dip ...

*They enter the water. The waters glug-glug a chorus or two. Biggins floats
and Moll supports his head*

(*Speaking*) Ah, Mrs Flanders, I am a poor sick man, and your company
gives me such comfort. In fact, I propose to move into the same lodging-
house as yourself.

Moll sighs deeply

I fear you are alarmed at the prospect?

Moll Oh no, dear friend, forgive me. I was merely thinking of myself and my financial difficulties. So selfish in view of your troubles.

Biggins I have been the selfish one. I had no idea you had money worries.

Moll Oh, yes indeed, dear friend. I shall soon be forced to beg on the streets.

Biggins God counsels charity in such matters. You see this little flap in my bathing suit?

Moll Why, yes. How very cunning.

Biggins Open it!

Moll (*demurely*) Oh, Mr Biggins!

Biggins No, no. Look! (*He opens it*)

Moll Oh! It's full of gold coins.

Biggins Take a handful.

Moll Me?

Biggins There's no-one else here. Give me your hand.

He gives Moll a handful of gold which she puts inside her costume

I can't have my little butterfly starving to death now, can I?

Moll Oh, Mr Biggins.

Biggins returns to the floating position

Biggins Ours is a perfect friendship. Mutually supportive.

Moll Have a rest, Mr Biggins.

Biggins Have a guinea, Mrs Flanders.

Both Thank you.

A musical vamp begins

Biggins What devil has put the following thought into my head?

Moll Mr Biggins?

Biggins Mrs Flanders, I should like to sleep with you.

Moll ceases supporting him and he "sinks" and comes up spluttering

I know it sounds improper.

Moll It is improper! Indecent even.

Biggins Only if we behave like animals.

Moll Oh.

Biggins Mrs Flanders, I want to show you my respect. I want us to sleep together like brother and sister.

Moll lets him sink again

Moll No, that's not a good idea.

Biggins	I meant no offence — you mistake my intents
	Our love will be pure as a babe in the wood
	I swear not to touch, and my illness is such
	Were I even to try, then I don't think I could!
Moll	But won't this bring strife to your marital life?
Biggins	I've the worst sort of wife that a man ever had!
	Our marriage went sour from its very first hour
	When I brought her back home and I found she was mad!

Moll (*aside*) It seemed cruel and heartless to refuse.

They get into bed

And old habits die hard. (*Aside*) Ladies and gentlemen, I'll be frank with you, to sin can be enjoyable. Sex as business and pleasure in equal measure.
Biggins I was swept away, ladies and gentlemen, on a tide of passion. I even got my health back. A fact that surprised me in view of the wrong I was doing.
Moll I had two children by him. We lived quietly and were happy.
Biggins Still, at least I could send the quacks packing ...

Ensemble	All men who are wealthy should try to stay healthy
	Of all the world's scoundrels a doctor's the worst
	'Cos in his profession the usual progression
	Is cut you up second, but stitch you up first
Moll ⎱	But we've no more need for this blood-sucking breed for
Biggins ⎰	We have a prescription for every disease
	Yes, true love can be a complete panacea
	Just take it at will with whomever you please
Company	Yes, true love can be a complete panacea
	It tastes rather nice and its action is fast
Biggins	She's thrown out my pills
Moll	And he's paid off my bills
Company	And all of our ills are now over at last!

There is a crossfade to:

SCENE 2

Biggins's house in London

Biggins is revealed on his sick bed surrounded by priests, doctors, lawyers, his mad wife and his four children. Moll stands apart

Song 15: Frail Man, Beware!

All (except Moll) Frail man, beware!
                              The devil seeks control
                              And torments he'll prepare
                              To mortify your soul

                              The kiss a whore doth sell
                              Should taste of sulph'rous coal
                              She'll suck you down to Hell
                              And damn your sinful soul

                              To cheat eternal fires
                              In Mother Church enrol
                              Before your life expires
                              Repent and save your soul!

Biggins I repent! I renounce her! I will never look upon her face again!
Priest Praise God; soon you will be free to frolic amongst the angels.

All   (*singing*) Amen

Underscore. Biggins writes a letter, with his wife dictating the key points

Biggins Madam, having been at the edge of the grave, I am by the unexpected
     and undeserved mercy of Heaven restored again. However, upon deep
     reflection on the nature of our mutual sin, I wish to renounce our friendship
     and desire that you remain in Bath. I enclose fifty pounds towards the costs,
     and furthermore request that you send our son to me to be brought up here
     in London.
Moll (*writing her reply*) Sir, dear sir. We have lived together six years. Will
     you not at least see me to say farewell? But, sir, since we are to part, I must
     have the sum of one hundred pounds. I find I cannot relinquish our son for
     any less. He is a dear boy — fit, and much stronger than his dear dead
     brother, our eldest. However, I undertake upon the receipt of a further fifty

pounds to relinquish any claims I might have upon his affections and upon
yours. Only remember me with kindness. Your Mrs Flanders.
Biggins Money, so it all comes down to money in the end.
Wife You're well rid of the impudent whore!

Music. There is a crossfade to:

Scene 3

On the road

Moll stands alone

Moll I have a hundred pounds then, as well as some moneys Mr Biggins gave
me during our time together and some few pounds sent by my mother in
lieu of a second cargo of tobacco. In all, nearly two hundred pounds.
Enough to live on for two years perhaps, but no longer. And, since I am
nearing forty-two, I must hasten to do what I can to improve my chances
on the marriage market. Once more to London then, and once more to
spread rumours.

Underscore

Landlord enters

Moll Landlord, have you rooms to let?
Landlord I do.
Moll I will take them, but I hope I may rely on your discretion?
Landlord Of course.
Moll Very well, I tell you this in strictest confidence. I am a widow with a
fortune in stocks and shares, all in my own name. Widows such as I are
much sought after on the marriage market, and, lest this knowledge fall into
the hands of adventurers, scoundrels and tricksters, I ask you to give it out
that I am poor. So, I beg you, keep my secret. (*Aside*) There is nothing like
a secret for opening a man's mouth.

Moll exits

Daisy enters

Daisy Landlord, who is my new neighbour?

Landlord Er ... she's a rich widow with a fortune in stocks and shares, all
in her own name, but I'm to give it out that she's poor because it's a secret.
So don't tell anyone.
Daisy I wouldn't dream of it.

Landlord exits

Daisy immediately begins writing a letter

My dearest Jemmy, at last I can show you in what affection I hold you. A
widow who pretends poverty for fear of adventurers has become my
neighbour, but I have it on excellent authority that she possesses a fortune
in stocks and shares ——

Moll enters

Good-morning, Mrs Flanders. Fine morning.
Moll Indeed it is.
Daisy But somehow it cannot compare with the sunrise in the north, where
my wealthy relations reside.
Moll Indeed? (*She promenades*)
Daisy (*continuing the letter*) I have made friends with her and am persuading
her to accompany me on a visit to Liverpool. All you have to do is to meet
us there and be introduced as my wealthy brother; I suggest the "estates in
Ireland too numerous to mention" approach. Then, make love to her, and
all your money worries will be at an end.

Moll returns to Daisy

I've enquired about coaches travelling north, and there's one tomorrow,
Moll. Would that be convenient for you?
Moll Entirely, for, once I have settled some business at the bank, I am at your
disposal.

She exits

Daisy (*continuing the letter*) My fee for all this will be one hundred guineas.
Your dear friend and lover, Daisy. PS We start tomorrow, after she has
conducted some business at the Bank of England.

There is a crossfade to:

SCENE 4

The Bank of England

The company are assembled

Song 16: Frail Man, Rejoice!

Company   Frail man, rejoice!
                   The Bank of England bold
                   Through strict commercial choice
                   Is content to save your gold

                   To get it you may kill
                   Your victim not yet cold
                   The Bank of England still
                   Will consent to save your gold

                   The Bank of England's law
                   Each client must uphold
                   Thou shalt not overdraw
                   For we've spent your wretched gold

Moll enters and approaches Clerk

Moll Excuse me, sir. (*She whispers to him*)
Clerk Fifty pounds? Well, that's not really an investment, is it? Look, I'm a busy fellow, far too tied up to advise on such trifling sums. But, do not despair, here comes Mr Honest, a clerk with a dangerous philanthropic streak. Perhaps he will assist you.

He exits

Honest Madam? (*He looks up at her and is immediately smitten*)
Moll I am a poor weak woman, all alone and seeking to invest some of my money, that it may bring me an income in the future. (*She hands him a bag of money*) But I fear my poor widow's mite is hardly enough to warrant your attention.

Song 17: Mr Honest at the Bank

Honest   Fifty pounds isn't much it's true

	But greater interest may accrue
	I'd take a sum of any size
	For the loan of a look from your lovely eyes
Moll	(*aside*) Another conquest on the way
	I'm glad that the dress was *décolleté*
	Although the sum is far from large
	Perhaps he'll invest it free of charge

She beams at him. Underscore

Honest I won't charge you for these investments, Mrs Flanders.
Moll How can I ever repay you?
Honest Ah, if only I were not married, Mrs Flanders ...
Moll (*aside*) Well at least he was honest enough to mention it.
Honest But, as it is, perhaps you could give me some advice?

> My wife is a demon sent from hell —
> She's twice as vicious as Jezebel
> She spends my money and drinks my wine
> But the bed that she sleeps in isn't mine

Moll	(*aside*) The world is full of married men
	And I'll never travel that route again
	(*To Honest*)
	Have you considered the natural course
	To sue her at once for a quick divorce?

The underscore continues

Honest Divorce? That's rather drastic, don't you think? And expensive, too.
Shouldn't I shoot someone instead?
Moll But the mess.
Honest True, and it's not as though I'd know who to shoot. The plain fact
of the matter is she has more than one lover.
Moll Oh, poor gentleman!

Honest	If I should do as you suggest
	And pluck this viper from my breast
	For all the money that I'd have spent
	If you were my wife I'd be content
Moll	Sir, we met but an hour ago
	And love requires more time to grow

	(*Aside*) Still, an investment might be wise
	And once we were wed his stock might rise
Honest	May I hope you'll not refuse?
Moll	A man may hope as a man may choose
Honest	Wait for me, Moll, and we'll vow one day
	To love, cherish, honour and obey
	I'll divorce that heartless whore
Moll	And I'll to the north in a coach and four
Honest	Keep in your heart the words we'll say
Both	We'll love, cherish, honour and obey

They kiss, tenderly. The underscore continues, building into the next scene

Moll And so we part good friends ...
Honest I to see a lawyer in Chancery ...
Moll And I to catch the stage-coach to Liverpool!
Honest (*waving and blowing her a kiss*) I'll write to you there.

    Honest exits

The Company "build" a stage-coach and board it as there is a crossfade to:

SCENE FIVE

On the road

Song 18: Stage-coach Song

Company	If travel should be your intention
	A coach is a wondrous invention
	Though we'd be more content
	If only they'd invent
	A less miserable form of suspension
	There's no chance of stopping for miles
	And it plays merry hell with the piles!
	The first half-hour is thrilling
	The second is frankly killing
	By noon you've lost a filling
	And, who knows, maybe added to which
	You could still end up dead in a ditch

The coach takes a perilous corner. The company cry out

Daisy	We're moving in fits and in starts, sir
	Which is hard on the intimate parts, sir
	And the man over there keeps polluting the air
	With some very malodorous farts, sir!
	But the truth is we don't really mind
	'Cos we're leaving the city behind
	The north is where we're going
	Where cleaner rivers are flowing
	And fresher winds are blowing
	So the man over there can go hang!
	Our journey will go with a
Moll	Our journey will go with a
Both	Our journey will go with a ——

There is a pistol shot

   Jemmy enters, masked and brandishing a pistol

Jemmy	Well, stand and deliver, my fine young girls
	With your pretty frocks and your flowing curls
	Hand over your rings and your strings of pearls
	Not forgetting that delicate brooch!
Daisy	(*reacting quickly*)
	My brother will have his small joke, I fear ...
Jemmy	(*fiddling with his mask*)
	My sight's unclear! Is that you, my dear?
Daisy	(*hissing*) The wealthy widow from London's here!

   (*Speaking*) Fool!

      (*Singing*) You've held up the wrong bloody coach!

Jemmy What? Is that you, Daisy?

Daisy Yes. And *that* is Mrs Flanders.

Jemmy It's this mask, the eyeholes are too damn small.

Daisy Just one of brother Jemmy's little jokes, Moll. He loves to dress up and impersonate a gentleman of the road. (*Aside to Moll*) Rich men must be allowed their harmless little eccentricities.

Jemmy Mrs Flanders! A name to tangle with. My apologies, dear lady, for any alarm I may have caused you. Will you be so kind as to let me make amends by consenting to ride behind me?

Moll I find myself delighted to accept.

Music (optional). Moll and Jemmy ride on into the sunset

The coach and the rest of the passengers exit

Jemmy Mrs Flanders, has me sister told you about me estates in Ireland?

Moll Only that they are too numerous to mention, and that on the finest of them you have a superior country house built after the manner of Sir Christopher Wren.

Jemmy Have I now? Indeed I have, I have. But I'm sure, Mrs Flanders, that me sister hasn't told you that your eyes are the colour of the wild Irish moors, where the purple heather competes for prominence with the livid green of the bog grasses and the velvet black brown of our rich sweet peat.

Moll No, I don't think she has.

Jemmy Or that your hair smells of camomile and dog violets. A woman of your great beauty, Mrs Flanders, would grace the natural splendour of me native isle. And I would here and now go down on me bended knees and beg you to be me bride were it not rather a difficult manœuvre on horseback.

Moll But are you not Roman Catholic?

Jemmy Ah, yes, so I am.

Moll It need not prevent us, sir, for I have such an affinity with your faith that I am willing to be baptized at any time.

Jemmy Well, that's handsome of you; we'll maybe combine the two ceremonies, your baptism, and a wedding mass to solemnize our union right afterwards, if that'll suit you.

Moll Excellently.

Some of the Company enter to see Moll's baptism and her marriage to Jemmy

Honest sings off stage

Song 18: Mr Honest (Reprise)

Honest (*off*)   Wait for me, Moll, for I'm almost free
And soon I shall have the divorce decree
Keep in your heart the words we'll say
We'll love, cherish and obey

The Company exit

There is a crossfade to:

SCENE 6

Liverpool

A bed and a chair are seen

Jemmy (*aside*) Ladies and gentlemen; sex as a highway robbery.

Song 20: Ride

Jemmy	So stand and deliver, my fine young flirt
	I'll have what's hidden there under your skirt!
Moll	(*mock prudishly*) Your liberties fill me with deep alarm
Jemmy	To fill you will be my delight
Moll	You speak very plainly
Jemmy	It's part of me charm
Moll	(*play-acting*) I'm all of a tremble
Jemmy	But not with alarm!
	Let's ride, let's ride, let's ride
	Till we've broken the back of the night

Jemmy makes a lunge at her, but she side-steps him easily

Moll	My jewel-case may be too hard to force
Jemmy	I'm not called Jemmy for nothing, of course
Moll	You're very sure of success, I see
Jemmy	I'm a divvil at breakin' in!
Moll	I'll give such a scream that the dead will arise
Jemmy	You've already raised something hard to disguise
	Let's ride, let's ride, let's ride
	To a place where you never have been

There is an instrumental verse, and Moll is playfully chased around the stage by Jemmy. There is lots of giggling, dodging, etc.

Moll	(*holding him at bay with a chair*)
	And what if the road you would ride is blocked?
Jemmy	Me powder's dry and me pistol's cocked!

Moll	What man would threaten a maiden so?
Jemmy	A desperate man, and more!
Moll	(*still play-acting*)
	Show mercy, I beg you, I'm down on my knees
Jemmy	I'll service you, madam, however you please!
	We'll ride, we'll ride, we'll ride
	As we never have ridden before!

There is another instrumental at breakneck pace. Moll and Jemmy indulge in more playful activity, this time rather hectic, with, perhaps, pillow-fights, water throwing, etc. Finally, they face each other, and the music stops abruptly as they gaze into each other's eyes

Jemmy	(*tenderly*) I'll treasure you, wife
	Sure, you'll not be misused
Moll	Be gentle ... (*pause*) tomorrow —
	Tonight you're excused.
Jemmy ⎱	(*alternately, then together, increasing in urgency*)
Moll ⎰	Let's ride ... let's ride ...

They manœuvre themselves on to the bed, where they are hidden from view by the head or footboard. The music takes over and builds up to a climax. Then it subsides

Jemmy ⎱	We rode like the wind and we rode with a will
Moll ⎰	A stunning display of equestrian skill
	Whoever thought that I'd
	Ever take such a wonderful ride
	Such a magical, wondrous, glorious, strenuous
	Ride

Jemmy Very well now, Molly, my love; all your gold, jewellery, bonds, investments and securities over my side of the bed.

Moll Dear husband, all I have is yours: twenty guineas. (*Aside*) I see no point in telling him of my London investments.

Jemmy Is that all?

Moll Yes.

Jemmy Are you sure?

Moll I'm afraid so.

Jemmy I've been cheated.

Moll Not by me you haven't.

Jemmy I thought you had money.

Moll I never said so.

Jemmy Christ's blood, that woman!

Moll Your sister?

Jemmy Me mistress more like, damn her. God in heaven what are we going to do? She's even robbed me of me last hundred guineas as her fee for bringing you up here.

Moll I've been here before.

Jemmy Oh, you make a habit of it, do you? Sweet Jesus, I might have guessed.

Moll No estates in Ireland, then? Not a single acre of rich sweet peat?

Jemmy Now, where would a highwayman come by that?

Moll Ah!

Jemmy (*seeing the funny side*) You play the fine lady excellent well.

Moll And I never met a finer gentleman.

Jemmy It's a shame neither of us have two pennies to rub together. Ah well, I absolve you of all our marriage vows.

Moll Thank you.

Jemmy A pity; we'd have made a fine couple.

Moll We would.

Jemmy But, now there's no advantage to be gained for either of us, we should separate at once.

Moll I suppose we should. (*Pause*) We still have twenty guineas.

Jemmy You'll need that. I could sell my horse.

Moll You'll need that.

Jemmy My wedding-ring.

Moll And mine. (*She hands him her ring*) You'd better keep them. You'll need them to give to someone else.

Jemmy That's true. (*Pause*) Farewell then, dear wife.

Moll Farewell, sweet husband.

They both hesitate

Song 21: The Hour is Late

	The hour is late, and I ought to go
Jemmy	But the night's so cold
Moll	Still I ought to, though
Jemmy	If things were different, then
Moll	Hush, I know
Jemmy	(*replacing her ring*)
	Well, take care of the ring on your finger

Moll makes to go

Ah, but don't go yet!

Moll turns hopefully. Long pause

	You forget your glove
Moll	You are kind, dear sir
Jemmy	That I am, dear ma'am
	Your eyes shine bright as the sun, my love
Moll	But it's late
Jemmy	Far too late
Moll }	
Jemmy }	To linger
Moll	The hour is late, and I must be gone
Jemmy	Though I'll always pine for those eyes that shone
Moll }	The road is hard that we're travelling on
Jemmy }	So may God and the angels speed you

Ah, my love, tomorrow's another day
And we all find happiness where we may
But think of me as you make your way
To wherever your journey may lead you

Jemmy Get away with you, now. I've a coach to rob.

There is a crossfade to:

SCENE 7

Mother Midnight's house in London

Underscore

Midnight (*aside*) Society abhors a whore. It requires women to be sober, virtuous and decorative, but how can they be when that same society encourages lasciviousness in gentlemen? It is the curse of our sex that we invariably end up bearing the fruits of others' temptation. This house is licensed by the parish for the lying in of ladies and the delivering of babies; and it is my misfortune to witness the sorry plight of many a poor woman caught in society's trap. I do what I can to help its sad victims, and, on account of the fact that many of the services I render are best performed under cover of darkness, I am called Mother Midnight.

Moll enters, heavily pregnant

Good-morning, Mrs Flanders, how are you today?
Moll A trifle heavy.
Midnight Well, here's another of those letters forwarded from Liverpool.
(*She hands the letter to Moll*)

Moll opens and reads the letter. Honest sings off

Song 22: Mr Honest's Letters

Honest (*off*)   The wheels of the law turn awful slow
                         And I'm still married but, even so
                         My heart is heavy and life is brief
                         To have you would bring me some relief

Moll (*bitterly*) There wouldn't be room in the bed.

She exits

Midnight Poor Mrs Flanders, the contents of her letter trouble her. Doubtless she will confide in me in the fullness of time.

Moll screams in labour, off

Midnight Rest awhile, dear, he's not ready yet. (*Suddenly remembering*) And here's another of those letters come on from Liverpool.

Honest (*off*)   Perhaps it's as well that you're not near
                         Or I might lose control, I fear
                         You'll never know how much I chafe
                         To place a deposit in your safe

Moll (*off*) Sweet Jesus, don't they ever think of anything else?

Moll's new-born baby cries

Midnight Mrs Flanders is delivered of a fine son; but still she seems troubled. Now is the time to offer her the benefits of my experience.

Moll enters rocking the baby

Midnight And how is he today?
Moll He so reminds me of my husband.
Midnight He's a little pet, isn't he?
Moll I miss him.
Midnight Why don't you write to him. Let him know he's a father.
Moll I don't know where he is.
Midnight Liverpool?
Moll No. When we parted, we agreed to go our separate ways.
Midnight That's inconvenient. How will you live?
Moll I don't know.
Midnight What you need is a new husband. From Liverpool?
Moll One whose letters are forwarded from there, perhaps.
Midnight Your baby's a problem though, isn't he?
Moll He's all I've got to remind me of Jemmy.
Midnight He might remind your new husband as well. Men always like to
    imagine they're the first. Or at least the only current one. Why don't you
    leave the baby with me; I'll find a nice cosy home for him in the country.
Moll A baby farm? No, I know those places. I might as well smother him now.
Midnight Are you calling me a murderess?
Moll No.
Midnight Are you sure? Do you know how many babes I've found homes
    for? Baby farm! Would I send dozens of helpless innocents to a cruel and
    undeserving death? The people I send them to are professionals. It's their
    livelihood to see them happy and well cared for, same as it's mine to bring
    'em safe into the world. Lord, Moll, they'll take better care of him than you
    will. Come, we'll go together to select a place for this little one. You shall
    choose his new home yourself. Oh, I almost forget, here's another of those
    letters come for you. (*She hands Moll a letter*)

Moll opens the letter and listens for Honest. Silence

Moll (*reading*) Good news! I will meet the coach to St Albans on Tuesday
    next, the seventh of July — that's today! — speed to my arms and ...
Midnight Leave him to me, dear, and good luck!
Moll Mother Midnight, I will never forget your kindness.

Moll gives Mother Midnight the baby and exits

There is a crossfade to:

SCENE 8

A Coaching house, then London

Honest enters clutching a pile of papers

Honest Mrs Flanders! Mrs Flanders! Moll!

There is the sound of a coach departing

Moll Mrs Flanders if you please, Mr Honest.

Song 23: Mr Honest's Death

Honest Oh, Mrs Flanders. But I've got to tell you my news, Moll ...

	Because ... the whore has gone where it's always hot
	My wife herself has untied the knot
	Her first good deed in her whole damn life
	Was to slit her throat with a butcher's knife
	She is well and truly dead
Moll	Does this mean that we can wed?
Honest	When these papers you have read
	We'll off to the Church and straight to bed

Moll But, Mr Honest, I can't marry you here. Not in a coaching house at the side of the road. Where should we sleep tonight?

The Publican and his wife enter

Publican's Wife Here, dear. We may only be a small inn, but we're friendly, and my husband and I will be only too pleased to give you our bed. I shall put fresh lavender in it, and I shall cook you a special breakfast with roast duckling and rhubarb flummery.

Honest (*aside*) How could she refuse? Ladies and gentlemen: sex as a reward for being a good boy ... I mean, sex in fair exchange for marriage and respectability. (*He unloads his documents and shows them one by one to Moll*) Proof of my divorce proceedings; proof of my wife's death, proof of the success of your investments, proof of my financial solvency and relative prosperity; proof of my continuing employment at the Bank of England, and an invitation to take tea with my mother at her residence in Hove.

Moll What more could a woman ask? I'm yours.

Honest At last.

They embrace

Moll I look at him and my eyes fill with tears. What an abominable creature
I am. And how this innocent gentleman is abused by me. How little does
he think that, having divorced one whore, he is throwing himself into the
arms of another. One that has lain with a quantity of men, and has had a
child since he last saw her. Poor gentleman.

Honest I love you, Mrs Honest.

Moll I shall be a good wife to you, Mr Honest. I will make you the happiest
man alive.

Honest (*aside*) And she has! She has! We return to London, two turtle birds,
where we live the delighted life of a happily matched couple. Until ——

Music

—— wretched man that I am, I one day hear that fabulous fortunes are to be
made by investing in a new company trading in the South Seas, and
recklessly involve our entire capital in the project.

Honest	And now, dear wife, the axe must fall
	The South Sea bubble has burst us all
	Our lives are squeezed in debt's cruel vice
	For now we're as poor as two church mice
Moll	Courage, husband, do not fret!
	Although we are mired so deep in debt
	What we have lost can be re-won
	Never give up till the race is done
Honest	What shall I do, now we're so poor
Moll	Do what the poor do, just endure
Honest	No, I must die, and join on high
	The glorious banker in the sky

An ecclesiastical choir take up the theme, off

Choir	So he must die and join on high
	The glorious banker in the sky

Honest dies

Moll (*aside*) With the death of Mr Honest, I must face facts. I am fifty. I am
penniless. My looks are gone, and along with them my source of income.
I am no better off than I was at five years old. Worse off; I have a child to
support, and it is now impossible that I should find another husband. All
romance and pleasure, all the satisfaction and excitement of being an object

of desire, are gone. What man would look twice at me now? One that is losing his eyesight, or his wits. Dear Lord, help me. Help me to find work. Without work the child and I must starve. God, sinner that I am, I don't want to die and he — the child — he has not even had a chance to live. Have mercy upon us! (*Pause*) Silence. Can it be he means us to die slowly? So be it; I shall say my farewells to life. I dress myself in my best clothes and wander round the city. London! Never has it seemed so full of life, of sound, of colour; so packed with people. London; where fortunes are made and marred before breakfast, where money changes hands as easily as a plate of hot buttered toast. London. Warehouses full to overflowing with delights from the four corners of the world. Barrels of wine, baskets of oranges, tubs of olives and salt pork. Old women selling prawns and lobster. The smell of fresh bread. In the taverns, men and women at dinner. Plates of roast meats, quails' eggs, bowls of sardines. Gravy runs in streams down their chins. I have no money. I cannot share in life. Am I already a ghost? A shadow?

Underscore and crossfade to:

SCENE 9

London. A churchyard

Moll I go into a churchyard to escape. Quiet and still. The tombstones almost friendly. Dull. Grey. Here lies Moll Flanders? Waiting. For the resurrection? For Justice? Mercy? I long for death. For the earth to open. To hear the rush of wings as the dark angel swoops.

A child enters

Child Jump; step; step.
Moll Who's that? Death's familiar? Already?
Child Jump; step; step ...
Moll No. A small human form. An elf maybe; or a goblin! A child's ghost.

The child stops, annoyed with herself for having got a step wrong

It is a child, a girl: the moonlight catching on some silver at her throat. The silver sets her apart, makes her look ... a child in a silver necklace.
Child Jump; step; step.
Moll (*to the child*) Lord, child, how you made me start! Don't be frightened.
Child You startled me!

Moll I'm sorry for that. Why are you here? This is no place for a little girl; no-one would hear a cry for help.
Child I live the other side.
Moll What are your parents thinking of?
Child No-one would hurt me in a churchyard.
Moll The world is full of evil people. They haunt places like this.
Child (*frightened*) I must go.

The music fades

Moll Trust me. I have children of my own. Show me your dance.

The child is nervous

We're friends, aren't we?

The child dances

I see.

Moll corrects her

Now.

They dance together holding hands for a while then stop. During this Mother Midnight enters and watches them

That's it! (*She hugs the child. Aside*) I could kill her and take the necklace.
Child I must go.
Moll Wait. Your hair is caught. Jump, step, step, step.

Moll marks the step as she fiddles with the child's hair. She unclasps the necklace and palms it

There. Now, off you go. I'll watch till you're out of this place.
Child Thank you.

The child runs off

Moll What have I done? Only taken the necklace. When I could have killed her. They will hang me if they catch me with it. No! I am not a thief. (*She* *covers her head with her arms and crouches*) Thief! Thief! Stop thief! I am not a thief. Not me. No.

Moll runs off in horror

Song 23b: Stolen (Fragment)

Midnight   Some people steal to survive for a day
             And some for a moment of pleasure
             But all of them know as they steal on their way
             The hangman is taking their measure ...

There is a crossfade to:

Scene 10

Mother Midnight's house

Midnight They say that fate's uncertain; but one thing a woman can be sure of is that when she passes forty-five her looks will wither faster than a spring violet. But, even so, I'm shocked at the sight of my former client, Mrs Flanders. Her skin hangs on her like an old petticoat.

Moll enters

Moll How is my son?
Midnight He's well, very well.
Moll Life has not dealt kindly with me lately, Mother. I am once more a widow, with another child. Can you place him for me?
Midnight Why certainly, I'll place him with his brother. But I'll have to charge you for him in advance.

Moll's face falls

     Or goods would do, instead of money.
Moll Would you take this? (*She produces the necklace*) A present from my husband.
Midnight A little on the small side, isn't it?
Moll Yes; he wasn't always practical.

Midnight Hm. Best if I buy this from you outright, I think, and dispose of
    it at once. If he was so "impractical", it might be stolen goods he bought.
Moll No, no, not stolen. How can you think that? He was an honest man.
Midnight It's a trade, Moll. Thieving is a trade like any other. And for poor
    women like us, it's one of the very few we can work at. You can be damn
    sure that the bankers and the lawyers and the churchmen and the fine
    gentlemen of commerce will not rub shoulders with the likes of us. Oh no!
    So if they will give us neither tools nor means nor hope of honest trade,
    why, then we'll take it when we find it. And in return they'll harry, hunt and
    hang us when they can.
Moll Damn them.
Midnight And on their side is money.

Underscore

Moll Damn their money.
Midnight Drawn from the trade of half the world, Moll.
Moll Damn their trade ...

Song 24: Damn, Damn, Damn

Moll	Damn, damn, damn
	This world of honest trade
	This world of trade be damned!
Midnight	Where the common coin is fear
	And gold alone is sure
	Where trade knows no frontier
	But the one 'twixt rich and poor
Moll ⎫	So damn, damn, damn
Midnight ⎭	This world of honest trade
	This world of trade be damned!

Midnight And on their side is law, Moll. Who can fight the law and win?
Moll Damn their law.

	Damn, damn, damn
	This world of honest law
	This world of law be damned!
	Where the one true judge you'll find
	Is the one on judgement day
Midnight	Where justice isn't blind
	It just looks the other way

Moll   ⎱   So damn, damn, damn
Midnight ⎰   This world of honest law
                    This world of law be damned!

Midnight And what can a poor *woman*, do Moll. It's men who have all the
   money and power in this world. What chance have the likes of us got. Might
   as well give up now, eh?
Moll No, no! Damn them all!

Midnight ⎱   Damn, damn, damn
Moll   ⎰   This world of honest men
                    This world of men be damned!
Moll   Where however mean his birth
                    A man may play the king
Midnight   And a woman's only worth
                    Is the dowry that she'll bring

Moll   ⎱   So damn, damn, damn
Midnight ⎰   This world of honest men
                    This world of men be damned!

Midnight Well, what can you do?
Moll I can sew.
Midnight Well, you'd better go back to your sewing, Moll. It'll ruin your
   eyes and pay you a pittance. Still, it's honest toil, my dear, honest toil.
Moll Damn sewing! Damn honest toil!

Midnight ⎱   Damn, damn, damn
Moll   ⎰   This world of honest toil
                    This world of toil be damned!
Moll   You pray to God for years
                    To send your daily bread
Midnight   But since he never hears,
                    Why not steal the stuff instead?

Moll   ⎱   So damn, damn, damn
Midnight ⎰   This world of honest toil.
                    This world of toil be damned!
Midnight   Shall we sink without a fight?

Moll No!

Midnight   Or gracefully withdraw?

Moll No!

                    We'll take what's ours by right

Midnight That's it!

Moll   Though it may not be by law

Midnight }   So rich men now beware
Moll   ʃ   Protect the things you own
                    We'll strip your mansions bare
                    We'll skin you to the bone

                    So damn all trade
                    Damn all law
                    Damn all men
                    Damn all toil
                    And damn, damn, damn
                    This world of honest sham
                    And honesty be damned!

Midnight If they catch you, they'll hang you; don't ever forget that.
Moll I shan't.
Midnight That's what they all say, so how is it the crows are so fat round
    Tyburn way? One mistake, Moll, just one slip, one piece of carelessness:
    that's all it needs. So learn to be frightened, learn to use your fear, learn to
    harvest it against the day you think you know it all. Oh, I'll get you teachers,
    Moll, the best there are, and you shall learn it all: pickpocketing,
    shoplifting, counterfeiting, for there's as many ways to cheat a man's
    money as there are to cheat his heart. Anything you bring me, I'll get rid
    of for a fair price, for I sit at the crossroads, where the traffic's busiest. So
    let's begin; it's time you met an old friend. Alice!

Daisy enters

Moll Daisy!
Daisy Daisy, Alice, what you will, Moll, so long as you whisper it.
Midnight Will you be her first teacher?
Daisy I don't know, Mother. I've not been well. (*She coughs*) This coughing,
    the fever.

Daisy continues her coughing and surreptitiously steals Moll's handker-chief. She coughs up some blood. Midnight and Moll assist her to sit. Moll searches her pockets for her handkerchief

Moll My handkerchief ——
Daisy (*producing it*) You've not got much to steal have you, Moll. Lesson one: never believe anyone who faints, has fits, convulsions, miscarries, is about to be delivered or coughs blood. We use 'em all for diversions whilst we're picking pockets or cutting fob watches. We work in pairs, and if someone drops down dead beside you, wait till they're sinking before you believe it. Come on, I'll show you.

Moll and Daisy exit

Song 25: Stolen

Midnight   Some people steal to survive for a day
                        And some for a moment of pleasure
                        But all of them know as they steal on their way
                        The hangman is taking their measure
                        You can bargain your soul for a morsel of bread
                        But none of your bargains will pay you
                        For of all of God's creatures there's none better fed
                        Than the worms in the earth where they'll lay you

                        Once I was fair as a morning in May
                        No-one could steal a heart faster
                        But the seasons have stolen my beauty away
                        For Time is one thief you can't master
                        Now I teach others to steal in my place
                        And my coffers with riches are swollen
                        But each morning I know as I look at my face
                        That each morning, too, has been stolen

                        Life is a river whose current is set
                        And you struggle against it in vain
                        But I'd die here and now, and without a regret
                        To be young for a moment again

She learns fast. Faster than any thief I've known. I'd say she was born to it; but thieves are made not born, and her whole life has been a preparation for her present profession. She's learned to make the best of herself, to take advantage of an unpromising situation, to watch, to wait, to pick her moment. The only difference is that now her talents are no longer in the service of others, but harnessed to a single burning purpose of accumulating wealth for herself alone. And I have never seen a woman so contented ...

Moll enters

Moll I learn to stalk the streets like an alley-cat looking for prey. It is so easy. I see a servant girl flirting with a shopkeeper, leaving her bundle unprotected. I take it. I see a silver tankard left carelessly outside a public house. I take it. I see three silver rings left on a window-sill. So easy to break the glass and take them. It is so easy ...

There is a crossfade to:

SCENE 11

Daisy's hanging

Underscore. A drum

Midnight Poor Daisy.
Moll It could have been me.
Midnight It still could be.
Moll It could be both of us. If she talks.
Midnight Who? Daisy?
Moll To buy a pardon.
Midnight But Daisy wouldn't ——
Moll Ssh!

Drum roll. Midnight mutters a prayer. The drum stops abruptly

Midnight Poor Daisy!
Moll Thank God.
Midnight How can you be so uncaring, Moll? Daisy was a good friend. She wouldn't inform on us.
Moll So it seems.
Midnight Well, neither would I. You're like a daughter to me.
Moll Even mothers have been known to abandon their daughters.
Midnight (*after a pause*) What will you do?
Moll Work alone.

Midnight exits

There is a crossfade to:

SCENE 12

A London street

Tradesman, Fop Judge and some of the Company enter

Song 27: I Shall Work Alone

Moll   I shall work alone
        And alone I'll face the danger
        For alone we live and alone we die
        And if I should hang not a soul would cry
        So on my tombstone carve in letters high
        "She worked alone"

Tradesman   When a man's in trade, then his livelihood's
        In danger from a person who can pick a lock
        So I bought a dog to protect my goods
        So vicious and so savage that your knees would knock
        But what a shock!

        For a robber came, Moll Flanders was her name
        And she stole everything that she could sell, sir!
        She emptied out the drawers, took the handles off the
            doors
        And she nicked the bloody dog as well, sir!

Moll   Since I've worked alone
        I have come to quite enjoy it
        Though I'm poor no more and my needs are few
        Still I couldn't stop if I wanted to
        It's nice to know there's something you can do
        So well alone

Fop   When a man with drink is fortified
        His mind will turn to pleasures of the female sort
        When I met Miss Moll I was quite pie-eyed
        So we turned into an alley for a moment's sport
        Or so I thought!

        She unfastened all my bows, put her hand inside my hose

Well, imagine how I must have felt, sir!
But it wasn't you-know-what that she whipped out like a
   shot
But the money in my money-belt, sir!

Moll   I and I alone
Could have done what I've accomplished
I'm the queen of thieves, I can safely claim
Moll Flanders now is a famous name
But still I'll search for ever bigger game
To hunt alone

Judge   When a man's a judge, as I'm proud to be
He should aim to support the law in every way
So when Moll Flanders burgled me
I should have told the constable the self-same day

But I never did resort to making a report
There was nothing I could really do, sir
For not only did she steal my robes and wig and seal
But she took my women's clothing too, sir!

All (except Moll) Well, she's put our noses out of joint
Her career we intend to check, sir!
She's stretched our patience to its breaking-point
But it's the hangman that'll stretch her neck sir!

Tradesman, Fop, Judge and Company exit

There is a crossfade to:

SCENE 13

The streets at night

*Cyril, very drunk, Moll, whores and various other low-lifes are scattered
about*

Cyril You! Woman! Over here.
Moll Is this fine specimen so blinded by his appetites and befuddled with
drink that he cannot tell the difference between an old woman and a young
one?

Song 27: Come With Me, Whore!/When a Man's Dressed Up

Cyril   Come with me, whore!
                     Let's find some dark alley
                     Where we two can dally
                     On Venus's shore

Moll Do you take me for a whore, sir?

Cyril I'll take you any way you want, madam. You see before you a squire; one up from the country, who hunts for his pleasure. Whose blood is fired by the spirit of the chase. Ever coursed the hare, madam, run, run, run, little hare, till your throat's ripped out and your death cry's sharp on the autumn air? A scream of ecstasy. To be blunt, madam, that's how I like my women as well.

Moll And your name, sir?

Cyril Robert.

Moll (*aside*) It is he. Cyril. But how can he use the name of his poor dead brother in these foul circumstances?

Cyril Is it not to your liking, then?

Moll No, sir, but names are unimportant for our business. If you will but remove your sword and follow me, I'll serve you.

Cyril   (*removing his sword*)
                     Oh, I'll make you sore
                     My fine young sprite
                     I may be tight
                     But I'll wager you're tighter

                     Let's tarry no more
                     My needs need fulfilling
                     And if you prove willing
                     I'll give you a shilling
                     So come, come, come, come lie with me, whore

Moll (*grabbing him roughly; aside*) Ladies and gentlemen: sex as a means to an end. In this case — revenge.

Moll and the whores begin to strip Cyril

Whores   When a man's dressed up for a night of play
                    His finery can make a woman's senses reel
                    "Oh, the food of love is divine", he'll say

And he'll promise you a banquet that'll make you squeal
Such a filling meal!
But when it's time for bed, and the finery is shed
Well, a girl can hardly keep from smirkin'
'Cos once he's bared his arse, the banquet's rather sparse
Two walnuts and a pickled gherkin

They finish manhandling Cyril

Whores }   Well, we did what we set out to do
Moll   }   And we took him down a couple of pegs, sir
                His tail was up when he first set to
                But it ended up between his legs, sir

The whores cackle dirtily and exit with Cyril

There is a crossfade to:

Scene 14

Mother Midnight's house

Midnight (*looking over Cyril's belongings*) You did turn him over. Even his stays. What did he do to deserve such rough treatment?

Moll I knew him. He once broke my heart.

Midnight I wonder you didn't kill him, then. Nice sword.

Moll What would I gain from that? If there was but one thing he taught me, it was always to put a price on one's passions. This way, we make a profit, and there is no hue and cry for his murderer.

Midnight Well, I'd better get rid of this lot as fast as I can. There'll be reward money out for it, I shouldn't wonder.

Moll Just so long as I make a profit.

She exits

Midnight (*aside*) And she does. Ten years she works at the trade. She becomes rich on it, and so do I. I tell her we should retire, we've made enough to live handsome for the rest of our lives, but it's no use; sometimes I think there isn't enough gold in the world to satisfy her lust for it. Every day she dresses in some new disguise, and every day she preys upon the city.

Boy rushes in

Boy Quick, quick!
Midnight What is it? Is the law after you?
Boy Not today, they're not after nobody today. They're all at the Old Bailey.
They've caught Moll Flanders.
Midnight What?

Music. There is a crossfade to:

SCENE 15

The Old Bailey

The Company are scattered about

Girl I saw her sir! My master keeps a warehouse. I saw her come to the door
of the warehouse and look inside. I was across the street so she didn't see
me, or the other girl what's in service with me. We saw her step inside and
we run and we comes to the door just as she was going out again with a great
roll of brocade under her arm. We seized her, we grabbed her. And we
shouted for help. We caught her red-handed. Red-handed! And if you've
got any sense you'll hang her to death.
Judge Out of the mouths of babes and sucklings.

Song 28: Hang, Hang, Hang

Company   (*like a baying pack*) Hang, hang, hang!
                      String up the cursed whore
                      And let the whore be hanged!

                      Let's hear her backbone crack
                      As she takes the final drop
                      Let's watch her tongue turn black
                      Let's see her eyeballs pop

                      So hang, hang, hang!
                      Let's send her on her way
                      We need a holiday

There is a crossfade to:

SCENE 16

Newgate Gaol

Moll is alone. There are voices from the darkness

Voice 1 Welcome to Newgate, Mrs Flanders.
Voice 2 Welcome home, Moll. Got here in the end, didn't you?
Voice 3 We've waited a long time for you, and here you are at last.
Voice 4 This is hell. Law-breakers always end in hell.
Voice 5 Caged like animals, crawling with vermin, stinking of vomit and gin,
waiting impatiently for the noose.

Song 29: Child of Newgate

Moll   Child of Newgate, child of darkness
                              Child of a dream that never could be
                              The rope is spun, my life is done
                              Tomorrow's sun is the last I shall see
                              Every sin I ever committed
                              Every crime, every hurt, every wrong
                              Each now stands a silent witness
                              To the fate I've cheated so long

This is where I was conceived. Where I was born. It is right I should end
my days here. This is surely divine justice. Oh God, in your infinite
wisdom, is this what you planned for me all along?

                              Who will mourn me? Does it matter?
                              All my life I've fought to survive
                              But, oh, the shame, the shame and the pity
                              To take my life when I feel so alive
                              Blind we're born and blind we struggle
                              And all we have is illusion and hope
                              But hope is just one more illusion
                              For all we find is the hangman's rope

                              Owls are calling
                              Night is falling.
                              I'm afraid

God forgive me my sins.
There is a crossfade to:

SCENE 17

The same

Jemmy enters, disguised as a priest

Jemmy I am a man of God, Mrs Flanders, come to pray with you before your
journey to the gallows. Let us pray together for the remission of your sins.
Repent, Mrs Flanders, so that your soul may depart your poor bruised body
and wing its way upwards like the lark towards that haven wherein resides
God's truth and justice. Tell me, Mrs Flanders, were you baptized?
Moll Yes, I'm a Roman Catholic.
Jemmy What!? Ssh! (*Whispering*) You are of the true faith? How can this
be? They told me you were born here in Newgate.
Moll I was, but one of my ... but my husband was of the Roman faith so I was
baptized into it.
Jemmy What was his name?
Moll Jemmy, a highwaym —— Er ... Jeremiah O'Highway was his name.
He had estates in Ireland too numerous to mention.
Jemmy Indeed. Mrs Flanders, God rejoices in the return of a sinner, and I
find myself so moved by your penitence and true contrition that I shall
petition the authorities to reprieve you. (*Muttering*) *In nomine patris et filii
et spiritus sancti.* Amen.

He starts to leave, whistling "The Hour Was Late"

Midnight enters

Midnight God works in mysterious ways.
Jemmy (*revealing himself as Jemmy*) And so do Irishmen!

Jemmy exits

Midnight (*to Moll*) Mr O'Highwayman! And I was searching for a priest!
Sometimes a successful imitation is more persuasive than the real thing.
Your sentence is commuted to ten years' transportation.
Moll To Virginia.
Midnight And we meet again at the docks.

Music. There is a crossfade to:

SCENE 18

The quayside and beyond

Midnight Don't worry, Moll, your money is safe, and I'll send it to you as soon as you're settled. But no more thieving while you're waiting for it. We are both too old for that game.

Moll Agreed.

Commotion off stage

Voices (*off*) Follow that man ... Stop thief! ... Catch him! ... String him up! ... He just stole me watch! ... After him! ... etc.

Jemmy (*off*) Wait. I have estates in Ireland too numerous to mention.

Moll I know that voice. (*To Midnight*) Buy them off. (*Aside*) And since Jemmy was responsible for my reprieve, it seems only fair that I should be responsible for his. After all, what are partners for?

Jemmy enters and they are reunited

Song 30: The Hour Was Late/Finale

Jemmy
The hour was late but the hour is past
And all rivers run to the sea at last
So hoist the mainsail upon the mast
There's a future that's ours for the winning

Moll }
Jemmy }
Ah, my love, tomorrow's another day
And we'll find our happiness where we may
But in your arms I can truly say
Every day is another beginning

Moll Ladies and gentlemen: sex as friendship ... and an alternative to playing cards on a long sea voyage ...

The Company assemble

Company
So the love-birds fly
To a land beyond the ocean
Buoyed up by their devotion

Far across the raging foam
And ten years go by
They make a tidy sum there
But, rich as they may become, their
Thoughts are never far from home

So they wave goodbye
To the mansion and plantation
To return in jubilation
To the England of their past
The storm was high
And the ship came close to sinking
But the harbour-lights are blinking
And the ship comes in at last

And Newgate's walls still stand
Like a blight upon the land
And its band of wretched sinners
Well, they go their wretched ways

Moll   But however dark the hour
There is still a greater power
It's the life that burns within us
That no prison can erase
That will set the walls ablaze

Company   So let's drink a round
To the seekers and the strivers
The against-all-odds survivors
And the heroes in disguise
Let the church bells sound
From each and every steeple
Ring a peal for the common people
For their spirit never dies

Let the church bells sound
For the daily grind
And all mankind
For their spirit never dies

Black-out

CURTAIN

FURNITURE AND PROPERTY LIST

Only essential furniture and properties are listed here, as mentioned in the text.
Further dressing may be added at the director's discretion

ACT I
SCENE 1

No props required

SCENE 2

Off stage:	Baby (**Man**)
Personal:	**Elizabeth**: gold coin, note

SCENE 3

No props required

SCENE 4

Off stage:	Stilts (**Mayor**)
	Stilts (**Nurse**)
	Ledger, pen and inkwell (**Nurse**)

SCENE 5

Off stage:	Brace of pheasants (**Robert**)
	Painting materials (**Artist**)

SCENE 6

On stage:	Broom, etc. for **Moll**'s chores
Off stage:	Second bag of gold (**Cyril**)
Personal:	**Cyril**: Bag of gold

SCENE 7

Off stage: Two babies (**Lady Constable**)

SCENE 8

Off stage: Letter (**Moll**)

Personal: **Luke**: lace
             Ralph: perfume
             Henry: apple

SCENE 9

Off stage: Letter (**Lucie**)

SCENE 10

On stage: Glasses, drinks, etc.

SCENE 11

No props required

SCENE 12

No props required

SCENE 13

No props required

ACT II
SCENE 1

On stage: Baths, etc.
             Bed

Personal: **Biggins**: gold coins

No props required

No props required

Personal: **Cyril**: sword

No props required

No props required

No props required

No props required

No props required

LIGHTING PLOT

Practical fittings required: nil
Various interior and exterior settings

ACT I, SCENE 1

No cues

ACT I, SCENE 2   Newgate Gaol

To open: Shadows and patches of semi-darkness

No cues

ACT I, SCENE 3

No cues

ACT, SCENE 4   Colchester

No cues

ACT I, SCENE 5   Lady Constable's home

No cues

ACT I, SCENE 6   Lady Constable's home

No cues

ACT I, SCENE 7   The Portrait

No cues

ACT I, SCENE 8   London

No cues

ACT I, SCENE 9   The Mint

No cues

ACT I, SCENE 10   A quayside public house

No cues

ACT I, SCENE 11   Sailing to Virginia

No cues

ACT I, SCENE 12   Virginia

Cue 1   **Elizabeth**: " ... my name before I was married?"   (Page 34)
             Evening effect as the scene dissolves to SCENE 13

ACT I, SCENE 13

To open: Evening effect

No cues

ACT II, SCENE 1   The pump room at Bath

No cues

ACT II, SCENE 2   Biggins's house in Bath

No cues

ACT II, SCENE 3   On the road

No cues

ACT II, SCENE 4   The Bank of England

No cues

ACT II, SCENE 5   On the road

Cue 2   **Moll**: "I find myself delighted to accept."   (Page 48)
             Sunset effect

ACT II, Scene 6   Bedroom scene

No cues

ACT II, Scene 7   Mother Midnight's house in London

No cues

ACT II, Scene 8   A coaching house and London

No cues

ACT II, Scene 9   London. A churchyard

No cues

ACT II, Scene 10   Mother Midnight's house

No cues

ACT II, Scene 11   Daisy's hanging

No cues

ACT II, Scene 12   A London street

No cues

ACT II, Scene 13   London streets

To open: Night time effect

No cues

ACT II, Scene 14   Mother Midnight's house

No cues

ACT II, Scene 15   The Old Bailey

No cues

ACT II, SCENE 16   Newgate

To open: Shadows and patches of darkness

No cues

ACT II, SCENE 17   Newgate

To open: Shadows and patches of darkness

No cues

ACT II, SCENE 18   The quayside and beyond

No cues

EFFECTS PLOT

ACT I

No cues

ACT II

Cue 1	**Chorus**: "Our journey will go with a ——" *Pistol shot off stage*	(Page 47)
Cue 2	**Moll**: (*off*) " ... don't they ever think of anything else?" *Moll's new-born baby cries, off stage*	(Page 53)
Cue 3	**Honest**: "Mrs Flanders! Moll!" *Sound of coach departing*	(Page 55)